S0-BYH-673

CONTENTS

22 DAYS IN NEW ENGLAND

THE ITINERARY PLANNER

ANNE E. WRIGHT

John Muir Publications
Santa Fe, New Mexico

For Randy, without whom this book would not have been possible.

Special thanks to my parents, Linda and Alex, for their research assistance and to Richard Harris for his support and guidance throughout the project.

John Muir Publications, P.O. Box 613, Santa Fe, NM 87504

First edition. First printing.

Library of Congress Cataloging-in-Publication Data

Wright, Anne E., 1959-
  22 days in New England: the itinerary planner / Anne E. Wright-
-1st ed.
     p.   cm.
  ISBN 0-912528-96-6
  1. New England—Description and travel—1981—Tours. I. Title.
II. Title: Twenty-two days in New England.
F2.3.W75   1989
917.4'0443—dc19   88-43536
                                                                                       CIP

22 Days Series Editor   Richard Harris
Design/Production   Mary Shapiro
Maps   Randy Johnson
Cover Map   Jim Wood
Typography   Copygraphics, Inc.

Distributed to the book trade by:
W.W. Norton & Company, Inc.
New York, New York

Your New England tour begins in Boston, Massachusetts, one of the nation's oldest cities, and ends there three weeks later after a 1,200-mile loop through some of the most scenic and historically significant terrain you'll find anywhere. Although this may not seem like a lot of ground to cover during your vacation, believe me, your 22 days will be chock-full of engaging activities, adventures, and picturesque sights.

New England is the birthplace of our nation in many respects. The pilgrims landed here in 1620, the first battle of the revolutionary war was fought on Massachusetts soil, Harvard University in Cambridge is the cornerstone of American education, and founding fathers such as John Adams spent their lives here. You'll feel history all around you as you pause on centuries-old town greens, drive past crusty stone walls that define property lines, ramble over covered bridges, and visit time-weathered historic homes and monuments. Along the way, you'll see where Shakers worshiped, poets penned, colonists rebelled, whalers toiled, and presidents were born.

Nature has also endowed New England with some spectacular landscape; Atlantic currents and ice-age glaciers have sculpted this part of the country to near perfection. During your holiday you'll have the opportunity to stretch out on sparkling white sand beaches, picnic in rocky coves, watch playful seals in their natural habitat, hike pine-covered trails, stand atop the highest peak in the Northeast, swim in bubbling mountain streams, dine on fish recently snatched from the ocean while you breathe in the salty sea air, and, if you're lucky, see the hills ablaze with vibrant colors as winter approaches.

This guide will open the door to your New England adventure. It has been organized for quick reference in an itinerary format divided into 22 daily sections containing:

1. A **suggested schedule** for each day's travel and sightseeing.
2. A detailed **travel route** description for each driving segment of your trip.
3. **Sightseeing highlights** (rated in order of importance: ▲▲▲ Don't miss; ▲▲ Try hard to see; and ▲ See if you get the chance).
4. **Lodging**, **campground**, and **restaurant** suggestions for each night of the trip.
5. **Helpful Hints**—random tidbits that will help your trip run smoothly.

6. **Itinerary Options**—excursion suggestions for travelers who have extra time.
7. User friendly **maps** designed to show you what the road up ahead is really like.

Why 22 Days?

For those who have about three weeks of vacation this year, "22 Days" itinerary guidebooks can help you use that time to the fullest extent by directing you to the best New England has to offer. How often have you wasted precious vacation time just trying to locate a decent restaurant or missed out on a treasured museum because you spent too much time in a disappointing one? In *22 Days in New England*, I've done the legwork for you so that your holiday will be as trouble-free and enjoyable as possible.

The itinerary, my ideal trip, includes a sampling of sights everyone should experience on a visit to New England, personal favorite haunts, and a realistic time frame in which to see them all. The daily schedules will help you structure your days but are not carved in stone. Use them flexibly to create the best trip for you. For instance, if art history is not your thing, skip the Boston Museum of Fine Arts on Day 2 and go to the Computer Museum instead, or spend the afternoon gorging on Fenway Franks at a Red Sox game.

What if you have less than 22 days? No problem. One of the nicest things about *22 Days in New England* is its adaptability. The itinerary is created for those who have three weeks, but if you only have one, pick the week that interests you the most.

The route begins and ends in Boston because it is the easiest point of entry for those traveling to New England from afar; however, the itinerary can be joined anywhere. With the compactness of New England, no stop on the itinerary is more than a three- to a three-and-a-half-hour drive from Boston, with the exception of Bar Harbor, which is about six hours. Those living in or near Boston can certainly use two- and three-day segments of the trip for a number of weekend getaways.

When to Go

This itinerary is designed for travel between mid-May and mid-September. Many historical sites, restaurants, and hotels listed are only open during those months when the climate is at its best. Of course, New England is known worldwide for its spectacular fall foliage, which generally reaches its peak in Vermont and New Hampshire in early October; winter skiing is also a popular attraction there. Do keep in mind that if you visit New England for the foliage or for skiing, many of the suggested sightseeing highlights will already be closed for the season.

July and August are the busiest months in terms of tourists and the most expensive—particularly in the coastal regions. Vermont and New Hampshire are naturally very crowded during peak leaf-peeping season, when places like North Conway in the Mt. Washington Valley of New Hampshire turn into veritable parking lots on Columbus Day weekend. If you plan to travel during peak periods, advance lodging reservations are a necessity. I've been told that churches have had to open their doors to stranded tourists or, worse, weary travelers have spent frosty New England nights upright in their cars. For your trip to run as smoothly as possible, I recommend calling ahead for reservations.

Personally, I think September is the best time to see New England. The weather is usually sunny and pleasant without the heat and humidity of July and August, ocean temperatures are at their warmest, and many sites are still operating on their extended summer schedules. You may miss the foliage at its peak (although I'll bet you'll see a few leaves turning in the northern regions), but you'll also miss many of the summer tourists, and off-season rates begin just after Labor Day in some coastal towns.

June is another good time to travel and avoid the crowds, but the weather is less predictable than in September, and high-season rates generally go into effect on Memorial Day weekend.

Transportation
Just about all of the principal airlines have several daily nonstop flights to Boston from most major U.S. airports. Prices vary depending on your departure city, but fares from airline to airline are generally comparable. Your travel agent can help get you the lowest priced flight available for your desired departure date. It is usually best to purchase your ticket at least 30 days in advance to secure the lowest fare.

While the metropolitan Boston area is readily accessible by public transportation and a network of commuter trains and buses, the rest of the trip is not. Greyhound, Bonanza, Peter Pan, and Vermont Transit bus companies serve the more rural areas of the itinerary to some extent, but you will find it hard to travel to all the sights once you reach each destination by bus.

This trip is designed for those traveling by car, RV, or motorcycle. With the exception of Sargent Drive along Somme Sound in Maine, all suggested routes are open to those types of vehicles. However, the auto roads to Cadillac Summit in Acadia National Park and Mt. Washington in New Hampshire may be too precarious for larger motor homes.

For aesthetic reasons, this suggested route follows secondary highways rather than major interstates in most cases. This means your average driving speed will be 45 to 50 miles per hour rather than 55 or 65. Distances between New England destinations are relatively short when compared to other parts of the country, so speed and travel time are not major factors in trip planning. You'll be able to appreciate the surrounding countryside better at slower speeds. You'll also find that states such as Maine, New Hampshire, and Vermont are very good about marking historical sites, lodging, and eating establishments that are off these secondary roads with directional and mileage signs.

Renting a Vehicle
All major car rental agencies have offices in Boston. Compact cars rent for about $150 per week with 700 to 1,000 free miles weekly. Subcompacts are somewhat cheaper and get better gas mileage but can feel cramped when you spend a lot of time inside them.

Traveling by rental recreational vehicle is another possible way to explore New England. Weekly rental rates for a compact RV that sleeps up to three people start at $620 during the peak summer months and only $380 weekly from October through March. A 20-foot or slightly longer RV sleeping up to five people rents for $680 weekly during the summer and $430 weekly off-season. These base rates don't include add-on charges for collision insurance, vehicle prep, propane, and the like. In Boston, RVs can be rented from Cambridge Rentals at 95 Brighton Avenue. Call them at (617) 437-7500 for rental information, or contact their parent company, CruiseAmerica, toll free at 1-800-327-7778. While touring by RV is a convenient way to travel, renting one will only mean significant lodging savings if you are traveling with more than two people.

Lodging
Country inns are one of the best ways to truly immerse yourself in New England tradition. Inns, some of which have been operating for 100 years or more, serve regional specialties, are often furnished with priceless antiques, and generally offer comfortable to exceptional lodging, sometimes at little more than the cost of a motel room. Lodging in a country inn averages about $75 per night for two during the summer and about $60 off-season. In many cases, the room rate includes a full breakfast, making the cost much more appealing, especially when you

consider that motels in the area average about $40 to $50 for two but provide only half as much in the way of amenities and atmosphere. For those who really want to travel lavishly, I have also listed luxury accommodations.

Camping is a much cheaper alternative to staying in either bed and breakfasts or motels, although many campgrounds on the itinerary are not as convenient to the sights. Campgrounds operated by state, national, and municipal park services usually charge less than private campgrounds—about $6 to $10 per night. Park-run campgrounds tend to be more wooded and less crowded than private campgrounds but often don't have facilities such as hot showers, grocery stores, playgrounds, or swimming pools on the premises as many private camping areas do. Of course, there is a price to pay for convenience: nightly rates at private campgrounds run from $12 to $18—or more. To get the most satisfaction from your trip, choose the type of lodging that best suits your life-style and budget.

Food

Preparing your own meals is the most economical way to eat on your trip, and you shouldn't have any trouble finding adequate provisions at any point along the way. If you're not equipped for food preparation or prefer to leave that task to others while on vacation, be prepared to spend at least an average per person of $3 to $5 on breakfast, $5 on lunch, and $10 on dinner when eating out. The restaurants I suggest are ones that I've personally enjoyed or that have local reputations for their food quality, uniqueness, convenience, or price. Fresh seafood is what comes to mind first when one thinks of New England cuisine, but places like Boston offer the visitor a wide variety in ethnic dining as well.

An ice chest or disposable Styrofoam cooler stocked with soda, juice, yogurt, cheese, and other snacks can save both money and time. If your bed and breakfast sends you off with a hearty morning meal, you can often get by until dinner with just a yogurt in the early afternoon. If your lodging establishment doesn't provide breakfast, a chilled fruit cup from the cooler may be just the thing to start the day. By cutting out one restaurant meal a day, you can reduce the total trip cost by more than $100 per person. Having the cooler will also save time, since you won't have to pull off the highway every time you feel a pang of hunger or thirst. Besides, the less time you spend dining, the more time you'll have to explore the New England you came to see.

Licenses
Since campfire and fishing regulations vary from state to state, it
is wise to check with each state prior to engaging in either
activity. Most states require fishing licenses (Maine sells theirs at
the Tourist Information Center in Kittery), and in some areas
permits are required for campfires.

What to Bring
Mark Twain once said, "One of the brightest gems in the New
England weather is the dazzling uncertainty of it." There
couldn't be a truer statement. The best way to deal with New
England weather is to come prepared. Even in the hottest sum-
mer months, it is possible to run into cool evenings in parts of
Maine, Vermont, and New Hampshire. Bring at least one heavy
sweater no matter what season you plan to visit the area. The
sweater will also come in handy any time you are out on the
Atlantic, whether it is on a whale-watching vessel, the ferry to
Nantucket, or a small pleasure craft; the ocean breezes can be
quite chilling.
   Although hopefully you won't have occasion to use it, rain-
gear is a must when traveling through New England. It is
unlikely that you'll be able to spend three weeks there without
encountering some form of precipitation, even if it is only a soft
island mist on Martha's Vineyard. I recommend packing a lightweight, hooded poncho to use while cycling or hiking and a
fold-up umbrella for city sightseeing.
   Binoculars will help bring the scenic vistas and wildlife of
Acadia and the White Mountains National Forest into closer
view, so make room in your suitcase for a pair. You wouldn't
want to miss seeing the seals bask on the rocks just off the
Maine coast.
   Also pack a small empty knapsack or daypack. It should be
large enough to hold your sweater, poncho, guidebook, map,
camera and binoculars and lightweight enough to carry easily
on your back. You'll find it invaluable when hiking, traveling to
the islands, or simply transporting a picnic lunch.

Recommended Reading
Reading (or rereading) *The House of Seven Gables* by Nathaniel
Hawthorne, *Little Women* by Louisa May Alcott, *Ethan Frome*
by Edith Wharton and *Walden* by Henry David Thoreau will
complement your New England sojourn as you visit the haunts
and homes that inspired these American literary classics. The
many layers of Newport, Rhode Island, society were the basis
for Thornton Wilder's enjoyable *Theophilus North* (recently
reissued as *Mr. North*), while Henry Beston spent a Thoreau-

like year in a tiny house on Nauset Beach in Cape Cod recording the passage of nature in *The Outermost House*; either book will add an extra dimension to your trip. Robert McCloskey's *Make Way for Ducklings*, a delightful tale of a duck family living in the Boston Public Gardens, will help the city come alive for young children.

As a supplemental guidebook, *The Complete Guide to Bed & Breakfasts, Inns & Guesthouses* by Pamela Lanier will help you locate that perfect country inn. Fodor's New England guide is a good background information source for those who wish to stray from the 22-day itinerary.

ITINERARY

DAY 1   Arrive in Boston and get settled in your hotel. Then put on your walking shoes—today you'll visit the *USS Constitution*, Old North Church, Paul Revere's House, and the Bunker Hill Monument, all stops on Boston's renowned Freedom Trail. Round out the day browsing through Quincy Market's smart shops, sampling delicacies from the market's main food hall, strolling along the nearby waterfront, and dining in one of the area's restaurants.

DAY 2   Today you'll explore Boston's museums. Isabella Stewart Gardner's Venetian Palazzo and the Boston Museum of Fine Arts are two of the city's most beautiful. At sunset, get a bird's eye view of the city from the Hancock observation deck, then have a late dinner along posh Newbury Street.

DAY 3   Cross the Charles River to Boston's sister city, Cambridge, and bustling Harvard Square. Harvard University's outstanding museums await art, history, and science devotees; or you may prefer to saunter through the college's ivied courtyards or amble past Brattle Street's stately homes, including that of poet Henry Wadsworth Longfellow.

DAY 4   Travel to historic Concord to stand on the site of the first battle of the revolutionary war. Take in colonial period rooms at the Concord Museum or visit the home of writer Louisa May Alcott. Picnic at Thoreau's Walden Pond. Then it's on to Lexington for the Museum of Our National Heritage.

DAY 5   There is more to hunt than witches in the beguiling city of Salem. Today you'll unearth some of the city's hidden treasures.

DAY 6   Driving along Massachusetts' "other cape," Cape Ann, you'll see the eccentric Hammond Castle and the fishing port of Gloucester, lunch by the sea in the artist colony of Rockport, and then continue up the coast to Kennebunkport, Maine.

DAY 7   Today you'll travel a large portion of Maine's celebrated coastline, passing through the picturesque villages of Camden, Rockport, and Wiscasset, to reach Bar Harbor by evening.

DAY 8   Glorious vistas atop Cadillac Mountain and the pounding Atlantic surf await you today in Acadia National Park, the easternmost U.S. National Park.

DAY 9   Give Acadia and Bar Harbor a last lingering look before you proceed across central Maine. After you pass through Gorham Notch, the scenic panorama of New Hampshire's Presidential Range from Mt. Washington's summit is the high point of the day. Late afternoon is for unwinding in Jackson or poking through shops and factory outlets in nearby North Conway.

DAY 10   Beautiful scenery abounds as you continue through the White Mountain National Forest. You'll see Crawford and Franconia notches, the Old Man in the Mountain, and perhaps hike the Flume Trail. Stop for the night in charming Woodstock, Vermont.

DAY 11   Enjoy Vermont's Green Mountains, picturesque villages, maple syrup, and delicious cheddar cheese.

DAY 12   Spend the day in the college towns of Bennington and Williamstown, viewing folk art by Grandma Moses in the morning and French Impressionist works, among others, in the afternoon.

DAY 13   The spartan life of the Shakers at Hancock Shaker Village makes an interesting contrast to the more traditional American life-style depicted in colorful oils at the Norman Rockwell Museum in Stockbridge. Today you'll observe both. A classical concert at Tanglewood or a modern dance performance at Jacob's Pillow caps off a memorable day in the Berkshires.

DAY 14   Travel southeast from Stockbridge into Connecticut and follow the Connecticut River Valley, making stops in Hartford, the state's capital, and the river towns of East Haddam and Essex. The night will be spent in the coastal town of Mystic.

DAY 15   Take a trip back into maritime history with a visit to the nation's largest maritime museum, Mystic Seaport. Then let yourself be entertained by thousands of aquatic creatures at Mystic's Marinelife Aquarium.

DAY 16   To get a glimpse of the greener grass on the other side of the fence, tour Rosecliff or the palatial Breakers, two examples of the lavish summer "cottages" built at the turn of the century by wealthy families such as the Vanderbilts. After the mansions, get a fresh breath of salty sea air along the Cliff Walk or stroll Newport's downtown wharf area where boutiques and boats entice the visitor.

DAY 17 Depart for Cape Cod, stopping in the whaling port of New Bedford. Visit Heritage Plantation and Sandwich Glass Museum in Sandwich, Cape Cod's oldest town.

DAYS 18 AND 19 Spend these two days bicycling, beach-combing, and window-shopping on the islands of Nantucket and Martha's Vineyard.

DAY 20 Return to Cape Cod and travel its length to artsy Provincetown. Explore the spectacular sand dunes of the National Seashore along the way.

DAY 21 You'll travel from spirited Provincetown along Cape Cod's scenic Route 6A to historic Plymouth, the site of the pil-grims' first settlement.

DAY 22 Return to Boston to end your three-week journey where it began, stopping in South Shore seaside villages and at the John F. Kennedy Memorial Library.

BOSTON

Your New England tour begins in New England's largest city, and one of the nation's oldest—Boston, Massachusetts.

Suggested Schedule

9:30 a.m.	Visit the public gardens.
10:00 a.m.	Begin your all-day tour of Boston's Freedom Trail.
1:00 p.m.	Lunch in the Italian North End.
2:00 p.m.	Cross over to Charlestown on the Freedom Trail to visit the *USS Constitution* and the Bunker Hill Monument.
5:30 p.m.	End your day browsing in Quincy Market's smart shops, then dining in one of the area's restaurants.

Arriving in Boston

Although Logan Airport is only two and a half miles from downtown Boston, getting to the downtown area can often be an exhausting experience. If you're renting a car, *don't* pick it up at the airport; wait until Day 4 when you are ready to leave the city and begin your trip up the coast. Cab fare will run at least $10 and can be very expensive if you get stuck in traffic, which you're bound to do. But a taxi may be your only option if you have a lot of luggage. Share a cab if possible.

If you're traveling light, the MBTA (Massachusetts Bay Transportation Authority) is the fastest and least expensive way to reach the downtown area. A free shuttle bus that stops regularly at all airline terminals will take you to the Blue Line subway. A subway token is $.60, and in ten minutes you'll be in the heart of Boston. Board the train on the "Inbound" side of the tracks.

Another option when traveling to downtown is to take the Water Taxi from Logan Airport. This is a quick and scenic method, but unless your hotel is located on the waterfront you'll still have to transfer to some other mode of transportation once across the harbor.

Amtrak trains arrive at South Station several times a day from New York and points south. South Station is on the main subway line, and no doubt your hotel will only be a short subway or cab ride away.

Greyhound operates a terminal in the city, providing access to

Boston from many smaller towns. The depot is near the Arlington Street subway stop of the Green Line in Back Bay.

By car, Boston can be reached from the west by the Massachusetts Turnpike, from the north by Interstate 95 to Route 1, and from the northwest and south by Interstate 93. The southern portion of I-93 just below Boston is locally known as the Southeast Expressway.

Getting Around

Walking is the preferable form of transportation in this compact city. Be sure to wear comfortable shoes, since many of the old brick and cobblestone streets were in place long before high heels came into vogue.

The subway system is the oldest in the country and sometimes operates like an antique. The network of lines (Red, Green, Blue, and Orange) is quite extensive in the heart of the city, but check your street map before hopping on a trolley. Often three stops on the subway are only three physical blocks apart, and it would take more time to wait for the train than to walk the distance yourself. The farther one travels from the city center, the more it makes sense to travel by subway, although it is best to avoid traveling them at rush hour. Tokens are $.60 each. In some areas, additional fare is required. Subway stations are marked by a "T" symbol. For your reference, all in-town subway stations have complete subway maps.

Since Boston has been settled for over 350 years, a great number of existing thoroughfares were laid down over old cowpaths that follow no logical pattern. The haphazard network of streets can be confusing to out-of-towners, and parking spaces are hard to come by. Don't try to demystify Boston driving or tame Boston drivers in three short days. Boston is meant to be enjoyed on foot.

Boston

Boston was established in 1630, and you get a sense of its long history the moment you arrive. It is hard to walk more than a block in downtown Boston without seeing some kind of historic marker. If it weren't for the parked cars, a walk at dusk along Beacon Hill's gaslit brick sidewalks and cobblestone streets might convince you that you'd traveled back in time to the nineteenth century.

With the exception of Back Bay, a former tidal marsh area that was filled in and laid out in the mid-nineteenth century, Boston's complex network of narrow streets, distinct neighborhoods, and old brick buildings give it more the feel of a European city than of a modern American metropolis.

However, one only need look at the number of glass

skyscrapers in the financial district to realize that progress has by no means passed Boston by. In addition to the thriving financial community, countless high tech firms have moved into the Boston area during the last 15 years, giving the economy a tremendous boost. Boston Harbor, once the city's mainstay, is still a busy port. Long a center for learning, Boston boasts one of the greatest concentrations of higher education institutions in the nation and is on the cutting edge of medical research. Consequently, Boston is an interesting, culturally diverse, and attractive city, steeped in its past yet vibrantly alive in its present.

Sightseeing Highlights

▲▲ **The Boston Public Gardens**—Founded in 1897 and designed by Frederick Law Olmstead, who also created New York's Central Park, these are the oldest public gardens in the United States. The gardens are in full bloom from April through October, but the stately trees and beautiful landscaping make the gardens a pleasure to visit in any season. Children will love the new "Make Way for Ducklings" sculpture, depicting a scene from the book of the same name, and a ride on Boston's own Swan Boats. A Swan Boat ride is a relaxing way for adults to get perspective on the city as well. The boats operate from 10:00 a.m. to 4:00 p.m. mid-April through mid-June and 10:00 a.m. to 5:00 p.m. mid-June through Labor Day (weather permitting). A ride costs about $1 for adults, $.75 for children under 12.

▲▲▲ **The Freedom Trail**—The trail is a three-mile walking tour of many of Boston's historical sites. It begins at the information booth in Boston Common along Tremont Street between the Park Street and Tremont Street subway stations. Sightseeing tours also travel the route. You can get tour information from the visitor information kiosk. Though the trail is well marked by a red line on the pavement, it is a good idea to get a Freedom Trail map at the information booth in case you decide to stray from the main route. The map also contains background information on each site.

The first stop on the Freedom Trail is the "new" **State House**, designed by respected architect Charles Bullfinch and built in 1795. The capitol was built on land belonging to John Hancock's family, and Samuel Adams laid the cornerstone. The State House can be toured for free from 10:00 a.m. to 4:00 p.m. Monday through Friday.

The next stop is the **Park Street Church** and **Granary Burying Ground**, where John Hancock and Samuel Adams lie buried near victims of the Boston Massacre. A little farther down Tremont Street is **King's Chapel**, built in 1754. Behind the chapel on School Street are the **Old City Hall**, now home

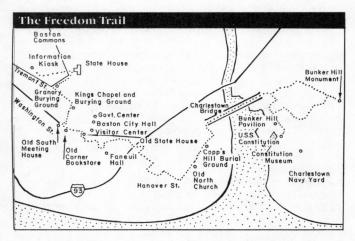

to a marvelous French restaurant, Maison Robert, and a commemorative statue of Benjamin Franklin. Several doors down on the corner of School and Washington streets is the **Old Corner Bookstore**, in a lovely brick building that dates back to 1712. Now known for its fine selection of regional and travel titles, the store is steeped in literary history; such notable literary figures as Henry David Thoreau, Henry Wadsworth Longfellow, Ralph Waldo Emerson, and Judge Oliver Wendell Holmes met there in the 1800s to discuss topics of the day.

Diagonally across from the Old Corner Bookstore at the **Old South Meeting House**, you can view a multimedia presentation on the building's role in history: Boston Tea Party rallies were held here. The meeting house was built in 1729. Admission is $1.25 for adults, $.75 for seniors, $.50 for youths ages 6 to 18. Hours are 9:30 a.m. to 5:00 p.m. daily April through October, 10:00 a.m. to 4:00 p.m. weekdays and 10:00 a.m. to 5:00 p.m weekends during the rest of the year.

The Old State House at Washington and State streets is the next stop on the trail. It was built in 1712 and currently houses exhibits on Boston history. Admission to the museum is $1.25 for adults, $.75 for students and seniors, $.50 for children six years old and up. It is open daily from 9:30 a.m. to 5:00 p.m. Just outside the State House is the site of the Boston Massacre, where five colonists were slain by British soldiers in 1770 foreshadowing the revolutionary war.

From the State House you'll pass through **Faneuil Hall** and **Quincy Market**, old buildings that have recently been refurbished to serve as a major focal point for entertainment, dining,

and shopping in the city. Return this evening for a more
leisurely visit.

From Quincy Market, cross under Interstate 93 to Boston's
thriving Italian North End. Visit Paul Revere's home before treating yourself to a memorable lunch in one of the North End's
fabulous bistros. The **Revere House**, built in 1676, is the oldest
building still standing in the city of Boston. Admission to the
house is $1.50 for adults, $1 for seniors and students, $.50 for
children ages 5 to 17. The house is open daily from 9:30 a.m. to
5:15 p.m. during the summer, 9:30 a.m. to 4:15 p.m. during the
winter, closed on Mondays during January, February, and
March. **The Pierce/Hicborn House** next door can be toured
with the Revere House for a combined admission charge.

After lunch, pick up the Freedom Trail again and visit the **Old
North Church** where the famed lanterns ("one if by land, two
if by sea") warned of the British arrival the night of Paul Revere's
ride. Farther up Hull Street, you'll pass the old **Cop's Hill Bur-
ial Ground** where Edward Hartt, the builder of the *USS Constitution*, was buried. Cross the Charlestown Bridge to the
Charlestown Navy Yard to view his creation, also known as
"Old Ironsides." The ship was built in 1797, saw active duty in
the War of 1812, and is the oldest commissioned warship afloat
today. There is also a *USS Constitution* museum, open year-
round. Admission is charged for the museum, but the ship itself
is free.

Just outside the entrance to the Navy Yard you can see a
reenactment of the Battle of Bunker Hill at the **Bunker Hill
Pavilion**. Reenactments are shown every half hour, and the
pavilion is open daily from 9:30 a.m. to 4:00 p.m. Admission is
$3 for adults, $1.50 for children ages five and up, $8 for families.
Then, walk up the hill to the 220-foot-tall **Bunker Hill Monument**, which commemorates that major revolutionary war battle. The monument is open from 9:30 a.m. to 6:00 p.m. June
through August and from 9:30 a.m. to 4:00 p.m. September
through May. Entrance to the monument is free.

As an alternative to retracing your steps to Faneuil Hall Marketplace on the Freedom Trail, MBTA buses that run frequently
from Charlestown to downtown Boston and the Faneuil Hall
area let you save your energy for a stroll through the market.

Lodging
Cosmopolitan city that it is, Boston has plenty of high-class
hotels to bathe you in luxury: the **Meridien** (617-451-1900), in
the financial district, the **Marriott Long Wharf** (800-228-
9290), and the **Bostonian** (800-343-0922) are adjacent to
Quincy Market; the **Ritz-Carlton** (800-241-3333), overlooking
the public gardens, is where visiting heads of state stay; the

Four Seasons (800-332-3442) is also adjacent to the public
gardens; and the **Copley Plaza** (617-267-5300) and **Westin**
(617-262-9600) hotels are in the Copley Square area. All offer
elegant lodging in convenient locations. Rooms typically start at
$170 per night, although many of these hotels have special
weekend rates beginning at $130 per night.

The **Lenox Hotel** at 710 Boylston Street near Copley Square
has less fancy accommodations at more reasonable prices
(617-536-5300). **The Chandler Inn** at Chandler and Berkeley
streets between Park and Copley squares has double rooms
starting at $70 (617-482-3450).

For simple lodging in an excellent location try **Beacon
Guest Houses** at 248 Newbury Street (617-262-1771). All
rooms have private baths and mini-refrigerators but only twin
beds. There is no maid service, but at $55 per night for two, this
is a bargain for Boston. Beacon seems to be the key word when
it comes to reasonably priced rooms: two establishments in
Brookline on the subway line which rent rooms in the $50
range are the **Beacon Street Guesthouse** at 1047 Beacon
Street (617-232-0292) and the **Beacon Inns**, operated under
the same management, at 1087 and 1750 Beacon Street
(617-566-0088).

The **Boston International Hostel** at 12 Hemenway Street
offers dormitory accommodations for only $10 per night. The
hostel is close to the Boylston subway stop on the Green Line,
Newbury Street, and Prudential Center and only a five-minute
walk from the Museum of Fine Arts. The hostel, which has a
fully equipped kitchen and showers, is handicapped-accessible
(617-731-5430).

To obtain a more complete listing of hotels in the area, call or
write the Massachusetts Hotel-Motel Association at 20 Park
Plaza #831, Boston, MA 02116, (617) 482-4414, for their free
lodging directory. If you are willing to stay outside the city,
you'll probably find a wider range of inexpensive hotels there,
but you will not have the convenience of the city at your
doorstep.

Dining

Boston has no shortage of good restaurants. Several that have
stood the test of time are the Locke Ober Cafe, Jacob Wirth's,
Durgin Park, and the Union Oyster House. The **Locke Ober
Cafe** (617-542-1340) down an alley off of Winter Street, established in 1875, is an old-money institution with dark wood
paneling, hard-backed leather chairs, and a men's club atmosphere. Prices are expensive. **Jacob Wirth's** (617-338-8586),
across from the New England Medical Center near Chinatown,
has changed little in the last 100 years. The wooden floors are

well worn, the home-brewed beer (both light and dark) is full-bodied, the hearty meals have a German flavor, and prices are moderate. **Durgin Park** (617-266-1964) in Faneuil Hall Market-place is yet another Boston tradition, noted for New England style meals, large portions, and surly waitresses. The restaurant originally served the men who worked the docks (big meals at low prices) and has tried to retain the same atmosphere, although prices are no longer dirt cheap. Just around the corner, the **Union Oyster House** (617-227-2750) has a raw bar and serves the best seafood in town. The restaurant was established in 1826. Entrées range from $15 to $25.

Anthony's Pier 4 at 140 Atlantic Avenue overlooking the harbor serves seafood on a grand scale. In size, Anthony's is more like a factory than a restaurant, yet it manages to maintain a pleasant atmosphere. Tasty dishes from the sea come with freshly baked popovers. If you have room for dessert, try the baked Alaska. Call (617) 423-6363 for reservations. In contrast to Pier 4's grandeur, the **Boston Sail Loft** at 80 Atlantic Avenue also specializes in seafood and overlooks the water, but in a crowded, yet relaxed, milieu. The Sail Loft's menu includes sandwiches, chowder, salads, and pub fare, with dinner prices ranging from $5 to $12. About a five-minute walk from Faneuil Hall, it is a popular night spot with local young professionals. Even more casual and crowded is **No Name** in the wharf area of the waterfront. What it lacks in ambience, No Name makes up for in low prices and the freshness of their seafood. Call (617) 338-7539 for directions, since the restaurant is hard to find, and be prepared to wait in line—they do not take reservations.

You'll be able to get fresh fish most anywhere on this trip. What you won't find elsewhere in New England is the variety of excellent ethnic restaurants that Boston has to offer. Try several of them while you're here. There are two **King & I** restaurants in Boston, one at 259 Newbury Street (617-437-9611) and the other at 145 Charles Street on Beacon Hill (617-227-3320). Both have the same menu offering delicious Thai cuisine, with dinner entrées averaging around $8. The spicy aroma of **Kebab 'n Kurry**, at Massachusetts Avenue and Beacon Street, can easily entice you into ordering more than you can possibly eat, and everything you sample will be delectable. The basement Indian restaurant is casual and offers affordably priced meals (617-536-9835). **Casa Romero** specializes in gourmet Mexican and Southwestern dishes. The restaurant, located in the alley just off Gloucester and Newbury streets, is open Monday through Saturday. Reservations are recommended, since the chef's talents are renowned in the area (617-536-4341). Prices are on the high side.

The North End is the place to go for Italian cuisine. **Felicia's** (617-523-9885) and **Villa Francesca** (617-367-2948) on Richmond Street are somewhat expensive, but the food, particularly at Francesca's, lives up to the price. **La Piccola Venezia** at 63 Salem Street serves traditional Italian specialties such as canneloni, manicotti, and lasagna. The restaurant is open Monday through Saturday (617-523-9802). Lunch or dinner for two will be in the $20 range. The ambience is red-checked tablecloth casual, as it is at **Sabitino's** on Parmenter Street, a bistro whose menu is similar to La Piccola Venezia. It is not unusual to see lines of people waiting outside these restaurants on weekend nights, since they do not take reservations.

Chinatown has a wide selection of Oriental restaurants, enough so that you can walk down the street and eat at whichever one appeals to you the most. Although I've never had a bad meal in Chinatown, my favorite is the **Lucky Dragon** at 45 Beach Street. For a spicy, inexpensive lunch, two people can share a single generous portion of the Singapore noodles (617-542-0772).

Ice Cream
As cold as the region gets in the winter, oddly enough New England has the highest per capita consumption of ice cream in the country. New Englanders are passionate about their ice cream! Almost every town on the itinerary has at least one ice cream parlor. You will be able to locate them easily by the trail of eagerly slurping patrons. Bostonians are connoisseurs and take their ice cream seriously. Hence a number of locally famous rival parlors vie for business. Wherever you decide to sample the sweet frozen dessert, you're bound to be pleased.

Steve's is possibly the best known of the lot and has locations throughout the area, including Quincy Market, Downtown Crossing, and Massachusetts Avenue in Back Bay. Try their mix-ins: crushed Oreos, Heath bars, chocolate chips, and the like, are hand-blended into ice cream freshly made the old-fashioned way. Their hot fudge sundaes are amazing. Steve Herrell, who originally founded Steve's and later sold the company, is back with his new parlor, **Herrell's**, on Dunster Street in Cambridge. **Emack & Bolio's** on upper Newbury Street also turns out a good product. For basic family-style ice cream, **Brigham's** operates several restaurants in the city.

A newcomer to the scene is **Il Dolce Momento** on Charles Street in the Beacon Hill area. Serving a range of unique Italian gelati flavors and sorbets, the parlor also offers tasty pastries and sandwiches such as chicken salad with artichoke hearts.

Boston Shopping
Boston shopping affords enough variety so that any visitor should be able to find what he or she is looking for. The best

shopping is clustered in five different sections of the city.

Newbury Street: This handsome street in the heart of Back Bay runs from the edge of the public gardens to Massachusetts Avenue and is home to the city's chic boutiques and art galleries. Sumptuous shops range from the trendy to antiques and traditional favorites such as Burberry's and Laura Ashley. One can find several interesting secondhand clothing stores toward the Massachusetts Avenue end of Newbury Street. Along the way, plenty of sidewalk cafés cater to weary shoppers.

Copley Place: This high-class shopping mall is an example of Boston's recent revitalization and gentrification. The Westin and Marriott hotels are at opposite ends of the mall. Tiffany's, Neiman Marcus, and Gucci's are all located here, as are an excellent newsstand carrying a wide variety of American and continental magazines, a six-cinema movie complex that features the excellent "Where's Boston" documentary film in one of its theaters, and a Rizzoli's bookstore. Saks Fifth Avenue and Lord & Taylor are nearby at the Prudential Center.

Downtown Crossing: This is the area of Washington Street one block east of Park Street station. Though not a visually appealing place to shop, the "World Famous Filene's Basement" is worth a stop, especially for bargain hunters. Barnes and Noble operates a large bookstore here, and fast-food addicts can have their fill at either The Corner or the fast-food hall upstairs at Lafayette Place.

Faneuil Hall Marketplace: The market is a good place to browse after sightseeing, since many of the stores are open until 9:00 p.m. The specialty carts adjacent to the food hall sell everything from Celtic souvenir shirts to batik sarongs.

Haymarket: This open-air fruit and vegetable market is held every Friday and Saturday alongside Interstate 93 between Quincy Market and the North End. Many of the vendors are true characters, and the market is a ritual that has remained unchanged through the years. You can get a hunk of brie cheese for a buck, and you may want to load up on fresh fruit and nuts for the trip. Beware: some vendors display gorgeous merchandise at rock-bottom prices but fill your bag with overripe fruit from the back of the pile. Make sure you pick what you want before you hand over the money. The best selection is in the morning, while the best prices are at the end of the day when the vendors try to unload their wares rather than carry them home.

Nightlife

If you're in a barhopping mood, the Faneuil Hall area is the best place to start because of the high concentration of drinking establishments there. **Lord Bunbury's** tries to capture the flavor of an English pub and draws a young, boisterous crowd.

Houlihan's is primarily a restaurant but has a dance floor that packs them in after dinner. **Cricket's** attracts the business-suit set, and **Lily's**, with a piano bar and outdoor seating, is a great place to people-watch on hot summer nights. Near Faneuil Hall, **The Black Rose** is a lively Irish pub, *the* place to go on St. Patrick's Day—if you can get in. **Tia's**, at the Marriott Long Wharf, is a summertime after-work favorite because of its outdoor setting.

Back Bay has a number of popular night spots, including **Friday's** on Newbury Street, which has a fun menu, tasty appetizers, and a crowded bar area where one can mix and mingle. **Daisy Buchanan's**, also on Newbury Street, used to be a Red Sox hangout but is now dominated by swinging singles. **The Elliot Lounge**, on Massachusetts and Commonwealth avenues, sports a relaxed and casual atmosphere. This is where the runners flock after completing the Boston Marathon. **The Top of the Hub** atop the Prudential Building has a terrific view of the city. The drinks aren't cheap, but the view is worth it. If your tastes run to Broadway show tunes, try the piano bar at the Lenox Hotel.

On Beacon Hill, one of my favorites is **The Seven's Pub** at 77 Charles Street. They serve great sandwiches with homemade potato salad at rock-bottom prices and have a good selection of imported beer. The milieu is smoky and very casual. The clientele is mixed but always friendly. Several blocks away on Beacon Street, **The Bull 'n Finch Pub** inspired the TV sitcom "Cheers." Although it has lost some of its neighborhood appeal to fame, it is still a fun place to go, especially if you are a fan of the show. For more elegant sipping, try upstairs in the lounge at **The Hampshire House**.

The Kenmore Square area is loaded with nightclubs that generally cater to a young crowd. Two of the most popular clubs are **The Metro**, at 15 Landsdowne Street, where you can dance to the sights and sounds of pop music videos, and **Spit**, next door, where punk music is the dance staple. If you like to dance to rock or new wave, you'll have to travel to the **Channel Club** at 25 Necco Street in the Ford Point area of Boston below South Station. Live bands perform there regularly.

Other: If a foreign visitor walks up to you on the streets of Boston and asks you "where is this place that you have war," he is probably referring not to the Bunker Hill Monument but to an area known locally as the "Combat Zone." The Zone lies between the theater district and Chinatown and is comparable to New York City's Time Square district. Although the Zone is shrinking, what remains is a strip of X-rated movie houses. It is best avoided.

Performing Arts

Music lovers should not miss the world famous **Boston Pops**, directed by accomplished composer John Williams, or the **Boston Symphony Orchestra**'s more traditional classical performances. Both make their home in Symphony Hall, except during the summer when the BSO travels to Tanglewood and the Pops give their annual Fourth of July concert at the Esplanade on the Charles River. Call (617) 266-1492 for ticket information. Boston also has its own ballet company, the **Boston Ballet**. The ballet performs free outdoor concerts at the Hatch Shell on the Esplanade in mid-August, and their annual presentation of *The Nutcracker* in December is a holiday favorite. Call (617) 542-1323 for their schedule.

The **BOSTIX** booth in Faneuil Hall sells tickets for all major theatrical productions. Check with them to see what's in town during your visit. It is sometimes possible to get reduced ticket prices there the day of a performance.

Sports

If you enjoy a good game of baseball, you'll especially appreciate watching one in Fenway Park, home of the **Boston Red Sox**. The ballpark's relatively small size makes attending a game more of a participatory, rather than spectator, sport. Call (617) 267-1700 for ticket information.

Wintertime visitors can catch either the **Boston Celtics** or **Boston Bruins** at the Boston Garden. Call (617) 523-6050 for Celtics information, (617) 227-3223 for Bruins information, and (617) 227-3206 for the Garden's schedule.

Racing buffs will be drawn to **Suffolk Downs** for horse racing or **Wonderland** for dog racing. Both tracks have their own stops on the Blue Line subway.

BOSTON'S MUSEUMS

The scope of Boston's museums is tremendous, from ancient Egyptian art to state-of-the-art computers, from an authentic Japanese house to lightning demonstrations, and from dolphins to European tapestries. Today you'll have a chance to uncover past civilizations and look into our own future.

Suggested Schedule

8:30 a.m.	Breakfast.
9:30 a.m.	Spend the morning exploring your choice of museums along the waterfront.
12:30 p.m.	Lunch in Chinatown.
1:30 p.m.	Visit the Boston Museum of Fine Arts.
4:00 p.m.	Visit the Isabella Stuart Gardner Museum.
Sunset	After dinner in Back Bay, visit the John Hancock Observation Deck to watch the sun set.

Sightseeing Highlights

▲ **Boston Tea Party Ship and Museum**—You get to throw a tea chest overboard in protest of the British on this replica of the eighteenth-century ship where the famous revolt originally took place. (The chests aren't actually filled with tea and are connected by rope, but at least you get to feel like a rebel.) The museum is open daily from 9:00 a.m. to dusk except for Thanksgiving, Christmas, and New Year's Day. It is located at 300 Congress Street on Museum Wharf, and admission is charged.

▲ **Boston Children's Museum** (▲▲▲ if you are traveling with children)—The museum is known for its hands-on exhibits, Native American collection, and Japanese home moved here painstakingly piece-by-piece from Kyoto. Children magically become hushed when they enter the Japanese house, but in the rest of the museum laughter prevails as they try on clothes in Grandmother's Attic, scramble up and down over several levels in the climbing structure, and blow bubbles as big as they are. Teens will enjoy "faultless jamming" in the clubhouse designed especially for them with electronic musical instruments that sound good together no matter how they are played. The museum is open daily from 10:00 a.m. to 5:00 p.m., Friday evenings until 9:00 p.m., closed Mondays from Labor Day through June. Admission is $4.50 for adults, $3.50 for children

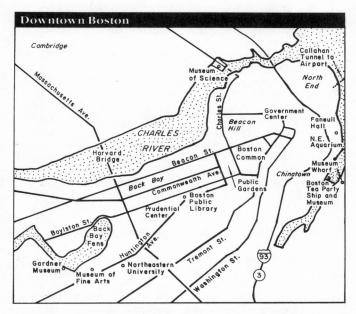

Downtown Boston

ages 2 to 15 and senior citizens. Admission is only $1 to everyone on Friday evenings from 5:00 p.m. to 9:00 p.m. The museum is located on Congress Street at Museum Wharf.

▲▲ **The Computer Museum**—With the influence of the high-tech industry in Boston, and nearby Massachusetts Institute of Technology turning out computer geniuses of the future, it is no wonder that Boston has the first museum devoted to the history of the computer. Get a close-up look at the first computers, then test your skills in the PC gallery. On Museum Wharf next to the Children's Museum, the Computer Museum is open daily from 10:00 a.m. to 6:00 p.m., Friday evenings until 9:00 p.m., closed on Mondays during the winter months.

▲▲ **New England Aquarium**—What trip to the coast would be complete without a look at the inhabitants of the sea? The aquarium has a magnificent cylindrical glass tank several stories high. You can views hundreds of species of sea life, including sharks, barracudas, and giant sea turtles as you wind down the spiral ramp. Dolphin shows are included in your admission ticket. If you don't have time to go in the museum, at least take a few minutes to watch the seals play at the outside entrance to the aquarium as you stroll along the waterfront. Admission is $6 for adults, $5 for seniors and students, $3.50 for children ages 4 to 15. Hours vary depending upon the season, but the aquarium is generally open daily from 9:00 a.m. to at least 5:00 p.m., later in the summer. Call (617) 742-8870 for current hours. The aquarium is located on Central Wharf, three blocks from Faneuil Hall Market Place, next to the aquarium "T" stop on the Blue Line.

▲▲ **Boston Museum of Science**—Test your strength, then discover the power of electricity. Learn about the earth's gravitational force, then explore faraway planets in the planetarium. One can spend hours in this fascinating museum unearthing the secrets of nature's unseen energy sources, as well as those that are visible to the naked eye, and how man tries to tame and control them. Many of the exhibits are participatory. The museum is open from 9:00 a.m. to 5:00 p.m. Monday through Saturday and Friday evenings until 9:00 p.m., except during the winter months when the museum is closed on Mondays. Admission is $5 for adults, $3 for children ages 4 to 14. Admission to the planetarium and Omni Theater is separate, and combination tickets are available. The museum has its own subway stop on the Lechmere branch of the Green Line.

▲▲▲ **Boston Museum of Fine Arts**—This is one of the most highly respected art museums in the country. The collection consists of ancient Greek, Roman, Egyptian, and Oriental art, with classic European and American artists represented as well; there are also American period rooms, early American furniture, silver, and fine musical instruments. The recently added West Wing, designed by I. M. Pei, houses changing exhibits, an attractive restaurant, and a superlative museum gift shop. Courtyard dining adjoins the lower-level cafeteria. The museum is open Tuesday through Sunday from 10:00 a.m. to 5:00 p.m., Wednesdays until 10:00 p.m. Admission is $5 for adults. Children under the age of 16 are free, and everyone is admitted free of charge on Sunday mornings before noon. The museum is located on Huntington Avenue across from Northeastern University.

▲▲ **Isabella Stuart Gardner Museum**—My favorite museum in Boston, this Venetian-style palazzo on the Fenway just two blocks from the Boston Museum of Fine Arts houses Ms. Gardner's extraordinary private collection. Imagine having a chapel with a thirteenth-century stained-glass window in your home and living with not one but three Rembrandts. Ms. Gardner, an avid patron of the arts, made it her life's work to amass this collection ranging from early Italian religious paintings to American and French Impressionists of the last century and beautifully intricate European laces. The courtyard, complete with Roman statues and mosaics, is abloom with flowers in every season and makes a splendid haven from the outside world. Concerts are given frequently in one of the halls, usually on Sunday afternoons at 3:00 p.m. There is also a café on the premises. The museum's hours are Tuesday through Sunday 12:00 p.m. to 5:00 p.m. There is an admission fee.

▲▲ **The John Hancock Observatory**—From the top of the John Hancock Tower in Copley Square, you'll see magnificent views of the city and beyond on clear days—and the city sparkles as night falls. The observatory is open Monday through Saturday from 9:00 a.m. to 11:00 p.m. and Sundays from 10:00 a.m. to 11:00 p.m. May through October; noon to 11:00 p.m. November through April (last entry 10:15 p.m.). Admission is $2.75 for adults, $2 for youths five to 15 and senior citizens.

Other Sights—You may wish to seek out any of a number of small museums that cater to special interests. The **Institute of Contemporary Art** at 955 Boylston Street features changing exhibits. The museum is open Wednesday through Sunday from 11:00 a.m. to 5:00 p.m. and stays open until 8:00 p.m. on Thursday and Friday evenings. The **Museum of the National Center of African-American Artists** focuses on visual arts by black artists. The museum is located at 300 Walnut Avenue. Hours vary, so call ahead for hours of operation during your visit (617-442-8614). The **Christian Science Center** behind the Prudential Building is architecturally interesting, as is the **Boston Public Library** several blocks away in Copley Square. The library was designed by the highly regarded architectural firm of McKim, Mead & White. Another library, **The Boston Athenaeum** at 10½ Beacon Street near the State House, is a long-standing Boston institution. The library's collection includes early American publications and an exhibit gallery of American art.

Itinerary Option
If your time in the Boston area permits, modify this itinerary to add a day trip to one of New England's foremost attractions, **Old Sturbridge Village**, a living museum that re-creates everyday life in an 1830s New England village. Candle making, blacksmithing, and woodworking are among the craft demonstrations you'll see there. Although children especially enjoy the village, adults will certainly be impressed as well. The village is open daily year-round, except for major holidays and Mondays during the winter months. Admission is high—$9.50 for adults and $4 for children ages 6 to 15—but the visit can be an all-day event. From Boston, take the Massachusetts Turnpike (Interstate 90) west to Exit 9 and follow signs to the village. The trip from Boston is about 60 miles each way.

CAMBRIDGE

Cambridge, like Boston, has been around for over 350 years. Remarkably, Harvard University has been in existence almost as long, and its influence is felt in just about every aspect of Cambridge life, particularly in bustling Harvard Square.

Suggested Schedule	
9:00 a.m.	Travel from Boston to Cambridge.
9:30 a.m.	Spend the morning on the grounds and in the museums of the nation's oldest university, Harvard.
12:00 p.m.	Lunch.
1:00 p.m.	Walk down Brattle Street as far as Fresh Pond Parkway to view Cambridge's loveliest homes. Visit the home of Henry Wadsworth Longfellow on the return trip.
3:00 p.m.	Spend the rest of the afternoon browsing through Harvard Square's many bookshops and boutiques.
6:00 p.m.	Dinner in Cambridge, then visit an area nightclub.

Travel Route
From downtown Boston, take the Red Line on the subway toward Alewife and get off at the Harvard Square stop.

Sightseeing Highlights
▲▲▲ **Harvard University**—The school is the oldest university in the United States. Its ivy-covered buildings and quiet courtyards (in some areas of the school) make it one of the prettiest as well. Stop in at Widener Library as you walk through "The Yard"; its collection is one of the most extensive of any library in the country. The library has a small exhibit depicting Cambridge history that may help put the city in perspective.

Harvard's huge endowment has given the school outstanding museums and innumerable buildings of interest. See if you can guess which one was funded by a major camera company (hint: it's near the yard). The **Fogg Art Museum** (32 Quincy Street), with its fine collection of Impressionist works, including a Degas ballerina, and Romanesque and medieval works, is my favorite Harvard museum. At the **Busch Reisinger** (29 Kirkland

Street), the specialty is German Expressionism. The **Sackler** (Quincy Street and Broadway), the newest of the Harvard museums, concentrates on Far Eastern and Islamic works of art. Admission is charged at each of the three museums. The museums are open Tuesday through Friday from 10:00 a.m. to 5:00 p.m., Thursday evenings until 9:00 p.m., Sundays from 1:00 p.m. to 5:00 p.m.

Also operated by Harvard are the **Botanical Museum**, with its unusual glass flowers exhibit, the **Peabody Museum of Archaeology and Ethnology**, the **Museum of Comparative Zoology**, the **Mineralogical and Geological Museum**, and the **Semitic Museum**. All of these museums are located on Oxford Street or Divinity Avenue. The Semitic Museum is open Monday through Friday from 11:00 a.m. to 5:00 p.m., Sundays from 1:00 p.m. to 5:00 p.m. The other museums are open Monday through Saturday from 9:00 a.m. to 4:30 p.m., Sundays from 1:00 p.m. to 4:30 p.m. Call (617) 495-1910 for museum admission charges.

▲▲ **Henry Wadsworth Longfellow House**—This was the home of poet Henry Wadsworth Longfellow for 45 years until his death in 1882. His major works were written here, among them *Hiawatha* and *Evangeline*. The house, built in 1759, has additional historic significance as George Washington's head-quarters during the siege of Boston in 1776. It is open daily except for Thanksgiving, Christmas, and New Year's Day and is just one of many beautiful homes along Brattle Street.

▲ **Mount Auburn Cemetery**—This is one of the most beautifully landscaped urban cemeteries anywhere. There's even a small lookout tower where you can view the surrounding cities of Cambridge and Boston. Charles Bullfinch (the architect who designed the Boston State House), American artist Winslow Homer, Henry Wadsworth Longfellow, and Oliver Wendell Holmes are all buried here. At 580 Mt. Auburn Street, it is a bit of a walk from Harvard Square but may be worthwhile if you appreciate historic tombstones.

Helpful Hints
The Cambridge Discovery Booth next to the "T" station in Harvard Square sells historic walking tour maps of the area for $1. The booth is open from 9:00 a.m. to 5:00 p.m. Monday through Saturday, from 1:00 p.m. to 5:00 p.m. on Sundays mid-June through Labor Day, and on weekends only through October.

Cambridge Shopping
Because of its proximity to Harvard University, Harvard Square has more than its share of bookstores. The **Coop** (Harvard

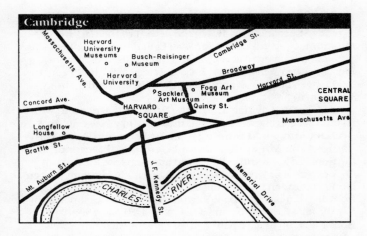

Cooperative Society), Harvard University's main bookstore, also
has considerable record and art print departments. **Words-
worth, Paperback Booksmith**, the **Harvard Square Bookstore**, **Reading International**, and the **Penguin Book
Shoppe** (the last one specializes in British imports) can all be
found in and around the square. You can browse to your heart's
content, since most are open late. It's a book lover's dream!
When you run out of bookstores, there are plenty of clothing
stores and specialty shops, particularly in **The Galleria** and
Charles Hotel shopping complexes, to keep even the most
determined shopper busy for hours. Don't miss the newsstand
in the center of Harvard Square; its selection of magazines and
newspapers is endless.

Dining

Harvard Square's restaurants run the gamut from fast-food
establishments to upscale bistros. **The Wursthaus** on JFK
Street serves excellent lox, bagels, and cream cheese, cold cut
platters, and a marvelous selection of beers from around the
world. Try **Yenching** on Massachusetts Avenue near the "T"
station for good Chinese food at moderate prices. **Au Bon
Pain**, next to Yenching, is the place to people-watch at outdoor
tables. Study chess players intent on their game as you sample
croissants in every flavor imaginable, gourmet sandwiches such
as tarragon chicken or chicken with bernaise, and creamy soups
from Au Bon Pain's kitchen for as little as $3.50 per meal. **Gren-
del's Den** (617-491-1160), at JFK and Winthrop streets, has a
terrific salad bar, good Greek combo plates, and a pleasant
atmosphere. Prices start around $6.

The Garage, on the corner of Mt. Auburn, JFK, and Dunster streets, is filled with out-of-the-ordinary fast-food restaurants. **Fromaggio's** creates unique sandwiches with fillings such as ratatouille and Boursin cheese on fresh homemade bread. At **Baby Watson's**, chocoholics must try the "chocolate orgasms"; the cheesecake is also pretty irresistible. **Cafe Aventura** serves great pizza for a song. **Leo's Place**, across the street, offers the best basic swiss burger and fries around. At the other end of the spectrum is **Upstairs at the Pudding** (864-1933) for fine dining. The "Pudding" is at 10 Holyoke Street, and reservations are recommended.

Two restaurants outside of Harvard Square that really let you experience other cultures are **The Middle East Restaurant** (354-8238) in Central Square and **Cantares** (547-6300) in nearby Inman Square. Both have fine food. The Middle East Restaurant obviously specializes in Middle Eastern cuisine, while Cantares serves Spanish and Latin American fare. Belly dancers perform at the Middle East Restaurant and live Latin American bands at Cantares.

Nightlife
Ryles Jazz Club in Inman Square has long been recognized as one of the Boston area's best jazz bars (876-9330). On Thursday nights you can see comedy upstairs at Ryles with Improv Boston. **The Regattabar** at the Charles Hotel in Harvard Square also has live jazz most evenings. **The Brattle Theatre** (876-6837) on Brattle Street in Harvard Square shows current art films, revives old film classics, and occasionally runs film festivals.

CONCORD AND LEXINGTON

The first shot in the revolutionary war was fired in Concord on April 19, 1775. During the hundred years that followed, Concord was home to some of America's foremost literary figures —Ralph Waldo Emerson, Nathaniel Hawthorne, Louisa May Alcott, and Henry David Thoreau. As a result of Thoreau's strong naturalist influence, parts of Concord have been set aside as nature preserves. Today you'll see what inspired writers to live in Concord. Then visit neighboring Lexington, which also has its share of charm and history.

Suggested Schedule

8:00 a.m.	Breakfast.
8:30 a.m.	Leave for Concord.
9:00 a.m.	Visit historic North Bridge, Sleepy Hollow Cemetery, and Great Meadows Wildlife Refuge.
11:00 a.m.	Tour the Concord Museum.
12:00 p.m.	Drive to Walden Pond for a midday hike, swim, and picnic lunch.
2:00 p.m.	Visit the Old Manse, Orchard House, Emerson's House, or the Thoreau Lyceum.
3:00 p.m.	Travel to Lexington to visit the Museum of Our National Heritage.
4:30 p.m.	Leave for Salem.
5:30 p.m.	Check into accommodations.

Travel Route: Boston to Salem (60 miles)
From Boston, take Storrow Drive west following signs to Fresh Pond Parkway and Arlington. Get on Fresh Pond Parkway and follow signs to Route 2. The entrance to Route 2 is two-thirds of the way around the second rotary.

If this is your first experience with rotaries, a word of caution: rotaries, circular intersections often found in Massachusetts when three or more roads come together, can be dangerous, so approach them carefully. A Massachusetts driver's advice on rotaries is, "Close your eyes and go." While this is not recommended, neither is timidity. Many unaccustomed drivers get hit because they hesitate too long. It is best to try to blend into rotary traffic as easily as possible, moving at a slow, but steady, speed. Do not stop in the middle of a rotary! If you miss your exit, just continue around the rotary and exit on your next circuit.

Once on Route 2 West, it's about a 15-minute drive to Concord. Follow signs to Concord Center. There is a tourist information booth on your left as you approach Concord Center.

From Concord, take Route 2A East to Lexington. You will cross Interstate 95/Route 128 before reaching the Museum of Our National Heritage. You may want to pick up fresh fruit for the trip at one of the roadside farm stands along the route.

From Lexington, take Interstate 95/Route 128 North toward Gloucester. I-95 splits off from Route 128 at Wakefield. Stay on Route 128 to Exit 35E, Route 114 East for Salem. The Lexington and Salem exits are approximately 20 miles apart. Should you wish to stay in Marblehead for the night, continue on Route 114 five miles east from Salem, then follow signs to Marblehead Center.

Sightseeing Highlights
▲▲▲ The North Bridge—On this site, British and revolutionary troops first clashed. Visit the bridge more for its historical significance than for what you'll see here today. The Minute Man statue stands at the site in memory of that fateful battle. The statue was sculpted by Daniel Chester French, whose grave is in nearby Sleepy Hollow Cemetery and whose home and studio you'll visit later in the trip. The visitor center on the hill above the bridge houses a gift shop and replicas of military attire that the minutemen used. The bridge is on Monument Street about ¾ mile from the center of Concord. There is no admission fee.

▲ Sleepy Hollow Cemetery—As you travel back toward Concord Center from the North Bridge, turn left onto Bedford Street. The entrance to the cemetery will be on your left. Follow signs to Author's Ridge. Ralph Waldo Emerson, Henry David Thoreau, Nathaniel Hawthorne, and Louisa May Alcott were all buried here, as was sculptor Daniel Chester French.

▲ Great Meadows Wildlife Refuge—This marshy area was frequented by Thoreau in his study of nature. Today you can follow the 1¾-mile Dike Trail loop and perhaps see a fox, muskrat or weasel in addition to the various species of waterfowl that nest in the wetlands. To get there from the cemetery, continue on Bedford Road for about ¾ mile, then turn left onto Monsen Road. Stay on Monsen Road to the refuge entrance.

▲▲ Concord Museum—The museum brings together Concord's military and literary histories. Items of interest on the museum tour include Paul Revere's lantern, which hung in the Old North Church in Boston the night of his famous ride, and personal articles of both Henry David Thoreau and Ralph Waldo Emerson, who were friends as well as fellow writers. The museum is open from 10:00 a.m. to 4:30 p.m. Monday through

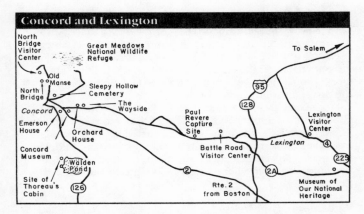

Concord and Lexington

Saturday and from 1:00 p.m. to 4:30 p.m. on Sundays. It is closed on major holidays. Admission is $4 for adults, $3 for seniors, and $1.50 for children. The museum is at 200 Lexington Road, just east of where Routes 2 and 2A meet.

▲ **Walden Pond**—Henry David Thoreau's famous retreat from "civilization" is now a popular escape for Boston city dwellers and their suburban counterparts. Being relatively mud-free compared to most ponds and much warmer than the Atlantic, Walden Pond is a preferred place to swim in the area. The pond can get crowded on a hot summer day, but the farther you walk from the main beach the better chance you have of finding a secluded pond-side picnic spot. There is a model of Thoreau's house next to the parking lot, and the actual Thoreau house site is about a ten-minute walk in from Route 126. The parking lot charges $3 per car and is the only legal spot to park within walking distance. To get to the pond, follow Walden Street from Concord Center south for about a mile. You will then cross Route 2, and the pond will be on your right, the parking lot on your left.

▲ **The Old Manse**—On Monument Street just below the North Bridge, the Old Manse was built in 1770 and was, at different times, home to both Ralph Waldo Emerson and Nathaniel Hawthorne. The house is open seasonally. Call (508) 369-3909 for hours of operation. Admission is $3 for adults, $2.50 for senior citizens, $1.50 for children ages 6 to 16.

▲ **Orchard House**—This was the home of Louisa May Alcott from 1858 to 1877 and the setting for her famous novel *Little Women*. Many actual furnishings are on display, including sketches done by an Alcott sister which still remain on one of the bedroom walls. The chapel in back of the house was built in 1884 as a meeting place for the Concord School of Philosophy.

The school was founded by A. Bronson Alcott, Louisa May's father. The house is open for tours April through October Monday through Saturday from 10:00 a.m. to 4:30 p.m., Sundays and holidays from 1:00 p.m. to 4:30 p.m. Admission is $3 for adults, $2.50 for senior citizens, $1.50 for children ages 6 to 17. The house is on Route 2A (Lexington Road) going toward Lexington.

▲ **Emerson's House**—Ralph Waldo Emerson lived here for almost 50 years until his death in 1882. Many of the writer's personal artifacts are on display, including a desk he used and part of his personal library. On Cambridge Turnpike just across from the Concord Museum, the house is open from mid-April through mid-October, Thursday through Saturday from 10:00 a.m. to 4:30 p.m., Sundays from 2:00 p.m. to 4:30 p.m. Admission is $3 for adults, $1.25 for children ages 6 to 17.

▲ **Thoreau Lyceum**—At 156 Belknap Street, the Lyceum is filled with Thoreau memorabilia, including a bookshop and library specializing in Thoreau's works and a replica of his house at Walden Pond. During the months of April through December, the Lyceum is open from 10:00 a.m. to 5:00 p.m. daily, 2:00 p.m. to 5:00 p.m. on Sundays. Call (508) 359-5912 for hours if you plan to visit in January through March. Admission is $2 for adults, $1 for students, $.50 for children grades 1 through 8.

▲ **Museum of Our National Heritage**—The museum is devoted to preserving all facets of America's heritage through changing exhibits that range from antique quilts to decorative arts to early military paraphernalia. It is open year-round, Monday through Saturday from 10:00 a.m. to 5:00 p.m., Sundays from 12:00 p.m. to 5:00 p.m., closing only for Thanksgiving, Christmas, and New Year's Day. Admission is free. The museum is located at 33 Marrett Road on Route 2A in Lexington.

Lodging

In Salem, the following inn establishments are all close to the main tourist attractions. The **Salem Inn** on 7 Summer Street (508-741-0680) is in an attractive, old brick building diagonally across from the Witch House. Double rooms and suites run from $70 to $90. The **Hawthorne Hotel** (508-744-4080), an elegant, small hotel on the town common, keeps company with Salem's stateliest homes. Doubles start at $90 per night. The **Stepping Stone Inn** (508-741-8900), adjacent to the Witch Museum at 19 Washington Square, is a cozy bed and breakfast with a cheery breakfast room and central location. The Salem Inn and Hawthorne Hotel both have decent restaurants as well.

Although you will be spending a full day exploring Salem

tomorrow, and the accommodations listed above are convenient to sights, you may wish to travel six miles further to the
charming seaside town of Marblehead for lodging tonight and
tomorrow night. A stroll down its winding streets, a seafood
dinner overlooking the water, and a drive out onto affluent Marblehead Neck are all excellent ways to relax after a busy day of
sightseeing. Two bed and breakfasts that overlook the ocean are
Spray Cliff (508-741-0680) at 25 Spray Avenue and **Harborside House** (617-631-1032) at 23 Gregory Street. Both offer
continental breakfast but only a few rooms, so reservations are
wise. Rooms at the Spray Cliff run from $85 to $110, while the
Harborside House is slightly less expensive. **10 Mugford
Street** is also a pleasant bed and breakfast, serving a buffet-style
breakfast in the morning. Double rooms are $60, two-room
suites with a private bath start at $95 during the summer and
cost $75 to $85 the rest of the year. Call (617) 639-0343 for
reservations.

There are no campgrounds convenient to the area.

Dining

In Salem, **Pickering Wharf** has the highest concentration of
restaurants, generally fast-food and take-out operations, ranging
from Chinese to pizza. **Victoria Station** (508-745-3400), also
at Pickering Wharf on the water, has outdoor seating in summer
and good steak and seafood dinner entrées that run from $10 to
$15. Lunch prices start at $5. The **Topsides Grill** and **Bull &
Finch Pub** also overlook the harbor at Pickering Wharf. The
fare at Topsides is mainly seafood, and the Bull & Finch is the
sister to the popular "Cheers" bar in Boston (508-744-8588).

In Marblehead, **Rosalie's** at 18 Sewall Street is the place to go.
Rosalie's delicious northern Italian cuisine is generally considered to be the best Italian food north of Boston. Entrées range
in price from $13 to $19, and reservations are a must (617-631-
5353). **The Barnacle** (617-631-4236) and **The Landing**
(617-631-1878) both overlook Marblehead Harbor and serve
fresh seafood. Prices are moderate to expensive. **Jacob
Marley's** at 9 Atlantic Avenue has something for everyone
on its varied menu. Prices are reasonable, and the atmosphere is
lively (617-631-5594).

SALEM

Salem is both beguiling and bewitching. It is a small city struggling to preserve its past glory while striving to keep pace with the twentieth century. The infamous witch trials of 1692 took place in Salem, and the House of Seven Gables immortalized by Hawthorne is here. Fewer people know about Salem's prominence in early America's foreign trade network. Today we'll examine all three facets of Salem's past.

Suggested Schedule

9:00 a.m.	Breakfast, then stroll past beautiful Federalist homes on Washington Square surrounding the Salem Common.
10:00 a.m.	Visit the Salem Witch Museum.
11:00 a.m.	Visit the Peabody Museum.
1:00 p.m.	Lunch.
2:00 p.m.	Spend mid-afternoon touring Essex Institute, the Witch House, a historic home, or just window-shopping.
4:00 p.m.	End your day in Salem with a visit to the House of Seven Gables.

Travel Route
Most of the day will be spent on foot. Use caution when driving in Salem's center. There is at least one intersection where six roads come together without so much as a stoplight, stop sign, or yield sign. The last time I was here, the most courteous driver in the intersection was a taxi driver.

Sightseeing Highlights
Salem—In 1692, mass hysteria gripped the city of Salem when several girls were said to have been bewitched by a West Indian servant named Tituba. This started a rash of accusations, and just about anyone exhibiting strange behavior was said to be a witch. More than two hundred townsfolk in all were arrested for allegedly practicing witchcraft. Nineteen of the accused were hung before Massachusetts Governor William Phipps put a stop to the executions in 1693. However, the events of 1692 were so traumatic that Salem is known, even today, as the "witch city."

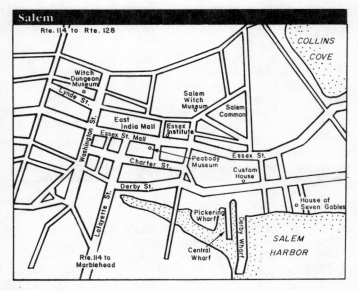

▲▲ **The Salem Witch Museum**—On Salem Common, the museum houses an audiovisual presentation of the events of 1692. It is an entertaining introduction to the history of the witch trials. The museum is open daily from 10:00 a.m. to 5:00 p.m., until 7:00 p.m. during July and August. Admission is $3 for adults, $2.50 for seniors, $1.75 for children ages 6 to 14. The presentation is shown on the hour and half hour.

▲ **The Witch House**—On the corner of Essex and Washington streets, this home is known as the witch house because accused witches were interrogated here by Judge Jonathan Corwin before going to trial. Built around 1642, it is one of the oldest houses still standing in the United States. Tour guides explain uses of eighteenth-century everyday household items and how expressions such as "sleep tight" and "turning the tables" originally came into our language. Admission is $2.50 for adults and $1.25 for children. The house is open seasonally, mid-March through November from 10:00 a.m. to 4:30 p.m. and 6:00 p.m. during July and August.

▲ **The Witches' Dungeon**—The witch trial of Sarah Goode is reenacted at 16 Lynde Street in a re-creation of the dungeon where alleged witches awaited hanging. Open daily from 10:00 a.m. to 5:00 p.m. May through November. Admission is charged.

▲▲ **Essex Institute**—At 132 Essex Street, the institute is comprised of a museum building containing a collection of art, silver, dolls, toys, and military artifacts from Essex County, plus four period homes, the oldest dating from 1684. The institute operates special witchcraft and Salem history tours during the summer. The last tour of the day leaves at 3:30 p.m. The museum is open Monday through Saturday from 9:00 a.m. to 5:00 p.m., Sundays and holidays from 1:00 p.m. to 5:00 p.m. From November through May the institute is closed Mondays. The admission charge varies depending upon whether you only visit the museum or tour one or more of the historic houses.

▲▲▲ **The Peabody Museum**—On East India Square at Liberty and Essex streets, the Peabody is a gem, with extraordinary depth for a small city museum. There are exhibits of nautical paintings, instruments, and ships' figureheads, as one might expect in a city whose livelihood came from the sea. However, the most fascinating exhibits in the museum are those devoted to goods brought back to this country through foreign trade. This collection includes fine china from the Orient, tribal artifacts from the Pacific islands, exotic furniture, silver, and even a miniature Taj Mahal carved in ivory. For children, there are several rooms devoted to natural history. The museum is open Monday through Saturday from 10:00 a.m. to 5:00 p.m., Sundays from 12:00 noon to 5:00 p.m., Thursday evenings until 9:00 p.m. Admission is $4 for adults, $3 for senior citizens and students, $1.50 for children ages 6 to 12.

▲ **Salem Maritime National Historic Site**—Run by the National Park Service, the site includes the Custom and Derby houses along with several wharves and warehouses illustrating Salem's former dominance as a port. It is open daily September through June from 8:30 a.m. to 5:00 p.m., and July 1 through Labor Day from 8:30 a.m. to 6:00 p.m. Located at 174 Derby Street, the site is free to all.

▲▲ **The House of Seven Gables**—At 54 Turner Street on the water, this is the house that inspired Nathaniel Hawthorne's well-known novel by the same name. It was built in 1668 and harbors a secret staircase. The house in which Hawthorne was born has been moved to the grounds in recent years, and the complex includes two other buildings dating back to the 1600s. You can tour them all from 9:30 a.m. to 5:30 p.m. July 1 through Labor Day and from 10:00 a.m. to 4:30 p.m. the rest of the year. Admission is $4 for adults, $1.50 for youths ages 6 to 17.

Salem also has many notable homes built in the 1600s through the 1800s which are open to the public, such as the **Ropes Mansion** several doors down from the Witch House on Essex Street. You will come across many on your own as you walk around the town. You can pick up a visitor map to help you locate them at the Chamber of Commerce in the town hall at 32 Derby Square.

CAPE ANN

Cape Ann is not as well known as Massachusetts' southern cape, Cape Cod; yet it is closer to Boston, and its more rugged coastline typifies, to many, the traditional New England coast. From Cape Ann, you'll travel through a small corner of New Hampshire before entering the state of Maine, or "Vacationland U.S.A." as it bills itself. Many of the most touristy areas in Maine are dedicated to the fine art of parting visitors from their cash; that's because many Maine natives make most of their annual income during the three summer months. Steer clear of the factory outlet meccas and enjoy the charm of quaint seacoast towns, the rocky shore, and the sweet smell of pine that permeates the air.

Suggested Schedule

8:30 a.m.	Breakfast.
9:30 a.m.	Leave Salem.
10:00 a.m.	Visit Hammond Castle Museum.
11:30 a.m.	Rockport.
1:30 p.m.	Lunch.
3:00 p.m.	Visit Plum Island and Newburyport.
5:00 p.m.	Leave for Kennebunk, Maine.
6:30 p.m.	Check in for the night.

Travel Route: Salem to Kennebunk (100 miles)
Today you'll be traveling along quite a few secondary roads that wind through small towns and at times take sudden turns making them hard to follow. Watch route signs closely to avoid getting lost. (However, if you have plenty of time, losing oneself on the North Shore can often be a rewarding experience.)

From Salem, take Route 1A North and cross the Beverly Bridge. Then follow signs to Route 127 North. Driving along Route 127, you'll pass through the lovely towns of Prides Crossing, Beverly Farms, and Manchester-by-the-Sea, where New England aristocrats hide their stately homes behind stone walls and vast lawns. Pride's Crossing railroad station has two waiting benches, one earmarked for Democrats and one for Republicans, adding a little humor to the morning commute. Often the most interesting homes and views are just off Route 127, so don't be timid—try out a few of the more intriguing side streets.

In Manchester, you may want to wake up with an invigorating

morning dip at Singing Beach, so called because the sand is said
to sound like singing when the wind blows. (A warning to non-
New Englanders: ocean water north of Boston may be a trifle
colder than what you're used to.) Parking at the beach is for residents only, but the ten-minute walk from town is a pleasant one.
Just be certain to park legally, for the police have no qualms
about ticketing or towing your vehicle.

Continue on Route 127 North to Gloucester, stopping off at
Hammond Castle on the way. At Gloucester, get on 127A North
to Rockport. An art colony for many years, Rockport has
become somewhat commercialized recently because of its
appealing seaside setting, yet the town still retains much of the
charm that originally drew the artists here.

When you're ready to leave Rockport, drive through Rockport center and follow Route 127 back to Gloucester. Four miles
out of town there is a turnoff on your right to Annisquam, a
sleepy hamlet with beautiful oceanside homes; this route offers
a quick scenic detour. Upon reaching Gloucester, take Route 128
South to Exit 14, then Route 133 North to Rowley. (Antique
lovers will be pleased to know that Route 133 is lined with
antique shops.) At Rowley, follow Route 1A North to Newburyport. From Newburyport take Route 113 West to Interstate
95 North. Continue on Interstate 95 North to Kennebunk, Exit 3
in Maine. Interstate 95 is called the Maine Turnpike once you
cross the Maine/New Hampshire state line.

The state of Maine operates an excellent tourist information
center, accessible from the highway, in Kittery just a few miles
over the state line. It's a good place to pick up a state map ($1)
and additional Maine tourist information from the helpful staff.

Sightseeing Highlights
▲▲ The Hammond Castle Museum—The castle, on 80
Hesperus Avenue in Gloucester, was built during the late 1920s,
although much of the building and its contents actually date to
medieval and Renaissance Europe. The castle was built for John
Hays Hammond, Jr.; though not a household name, he holds
over 400 patents and is credited with many inventions that have
shaped modern life, ranging from radio control systems to shav-
ing cream. The castle interior includes an organ with over 8,000
pipes and, in the center of a medieval courtyard, a reflecting
pool into which Mr. Hammond used to dive from his second-
floor bedroom window. Another unique fixture in the castle is a
rainmaking system, which Hammond installed in the roof over
the courtyard to water his plants. On Route 127, the turnoff to
Hesperus Avenue is about 4½ miles from Manchester Center on
your right. The street sign is not well marked from this direction, so keep your eyes peeled. Guided tours are $3.50 for

adults, $3 for students and senior citizens, $2 for children ages 6 to 12. The castle should be open daily from 10:00 a.m. to 4:00 p.m., but you may want to call ahead (508-283-2080) to verify hours during your visit, as their hours seem somewhat sporadic.

▲▲ **Plum Island and Parker River National Wildlife Refuge**—This stop on the itinerary offers car-cramped legs miles of white sand beaches to walk on and bird-watchers an opportunity to see various species in their natural habitat. Admission is free, although the number of cars entering the refuge is sometimes restricted for environmental reasons. To get there, turn right onto Rolfe's Lane from 1A in Newbury and follow the signs. One word of caution: in early July, the beaches in this area are visited by "greenheads," a type of horsefly with a nasty bite. The greenhead season only lasts about two weeks, and I've been told bug spray will repel them. Come prepared and you can still appreciate this beautiful park.

Lodging
When it comes to eating and sleeping, Kennebunkport gets more tourist traffic than Kennebunk, which means crowds and

higher prices. I recommend staying in the quieter Kennebunk, which is also closer to the highway. **The Kennebunk Inn** on Main Street in Kennebunk center, built in 1799, is as comfortable and charming as anything you'll find in neighboring Kennebunkport and less costly. Double rooms average about $65 per night at the height of the summer season and significantly less in the off-season. With the exception of Christmas Day, the inn is open year-round. There is also an excellent restaurant on the premises. Call (207) 985-3351 for reservations.

As a last resort, stay at one of the two motels on opposite sides of Exit 3. They take advantage of the overflow from Kennebunkport, so their rates are just about as high and even higher than the Kennebunk Inn's but without the ambience.

Camping
Yankeeland Campground is less than three miles from Interstate 95. Get off I-95 North at Exit 3; a right turn at the end of the exit ramp will take you in the opposite direction from Kennebunk. Drive straight for 2.7 miles. The entrance to the campground will be on your left. Hookups, hot showers, and complete recreational facilities, including swimming, are all available. The campground is open from May through Columbus Day. For reservations call (207) 985-7576.

Dining
For lunch, I recommend **Woodman's** on the causeway in Essex about three miles after turning onto Route 133. Woodman's is a North Shore institution serving phenomenal fried clams. Although their prices are no longer dirt cheap, portions are so large that two people should have no problem splitting a dinner. If hunger sets in before you leave Rockport, there are plenty of restaurants on Bearskin Neck or along Beach Street in the center of town.

For your evening meal in Kennebunk, **Squaretoes** on Main Street offers traditional Italian, New England, and seafood dishes at moderate prices. They also serve decent breakfasts.

The Kennebunk Inn across the street is the place to go for more refined dining. Haddock Chablis, shrimp Louisiana, and scallops with peaches are just a few of their unusual seafood offerings.

Itinerary Options
Cape Ann, with its quiet towns and excellent beaches, is a relaxing place to unwind for a few days. Cranes Beach off Route 133 in Ipswich and Good Harbor Beach off Route 127 in Gloucester are two of my favorite beaches in the area. The parking lot at Good Harbor is for residents only, but sometimes you can find

parking within walking distance. For a fee, anyone can park at Crane's. On hot summer days, especially weekends, the lot fills up quickly. The Crane Mansion at nearby Castle Hill was built with money made in bathroom fixtures and is now rented out for elegant parties.

Picnics and polo go hand in hand at the Myopia Hunt Club. The action usually starts around 3:00 p.m. on Sunday afternoons throughout the summer and early fall. The polo grounds are off Route 1A in Hamilton. Call (508) 468-7956 for information.

Summer whale-watching expeditions are a very popular North Shore pastime. The Yankee Fleet in Gloucester operates both whale-watching cruises and deep-sea fishing trips. Call (800) WHALING or (508) 283-0313 for prices and schedules.

If you do stick around the North Shore for awhile, Chipper's River Cafe (508-356-7956) on Market Street in Ipswich has delicious, out-of-the-ordinary sandwiches at reasonable prices. The Wenham Tea House (508-468-1398) serves simple home-cooked meals and cornbread that will carry you back to your childhood.

Exit 7 off Interstate 95, about 20 miles north of the center of Newburyport, will take you to historic downtown Portsmouth, New Hampshire. Many New Englanders stop here just to visit the famous Blue Strawberry restaurant, which serves fabulous six-course dinners. The Blue Strawberry is at 29 Ceres Street overlooking the harbor, and reservations are required (603-431-6420).

COASTAL MAINE

The object of the day is to travel from Kennebunk to Bar Harbor, about a four-and-a-half-hour drive, much of it along Maine's scenic coastline. The best way to enjoy the trip is to follow the travel route at your own pace, seeing what interests you most. Whether it's browsing through Kennebunkport's shops or swimming at Kennebunk Beach in the morning, outlet shopping in Freeport, viewing fine art at the Portland Museum of Art, or picnicking on the harbor in lovely Camden, the day invites you to spend it at your leisure.

Suggested Schedule	
9:00 a.m.	Leave Kennebunk.
6:00 p.m.	Arrive in Bar Harbor.

Travel Route: Kennebunk to Bar Harbor (200 miles)
Take the Maine Turnpike (Interstate 95) north from Kennebunk. If you wish to make a stop in Portland, take Exit 6A and get onto Interstate 295; otherwise continue on 95 North. Although Portland is Maine's largest city, it is still small enough that any exit for downtown will take you to the center of Portland as long as you drive east. The Old Port Exchange District on the waterfront is being revitalized, and the Portland Art Museum at Congress and High streets has a wonderful collection of Winslow Homer paintings and is well respected in art circles. Interstate 295 will take you back to the turnpike if you just continue north.

Fans of L. L. Bean and designer outlets might want to stop in the once-sleepy town of Freeport, now a mile-long strip of names like Ralph Lauren, Anne Klein, and Benetton. Good bargains can be found, and a midnight shopping spree at L. L. Bean (open 24 hours) is a rite of passage for any New England college student. To stop in Freeport, take Exit 19 off the turnpike. You can shop your way through Freeport and get right back on the highway at the other end of town, Exit 20.

Everyone should exit the turnpike at Exit 22 for Bath, Brunswick, and coastal Route 1. Follow Route 1 all the way up to Ellsworth, passing through the towns of Wiscasset ("the prettiest town in Maine"), Rockport (nestled in a quiet cove about one mile off Route l), and Camden (with its harbor park overlooking

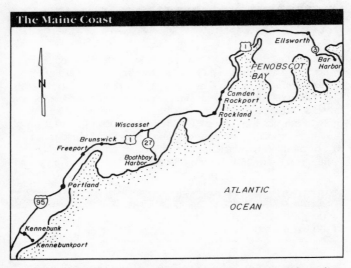

Penobscot Bay). The drive from Freeport to Camden takes a little under two hours without stops, and it is another hour and a
half from Camden to Bar Harbor. From Rockport on, you'll
catch tantalizing glimpses of the sea all along the route. Flea
market buffs will find Route 1 in Searsport absolute heaven.
Those with extra time may fancy a detour onto Route 27 East
and the Boothbay Peninsula, where scenic coves, quaint shops,
and art galleries await visitors.

At Ellsworth, take Route 3 East for the final twenty-mile leg of
the journey to Bar Harbor.

Lodging
For my money, **McKay's Cottages** (207-288-3531) on Main
Street in Bar Harbor and **Daney's Cottage** (207-288-3856),
one-half block away on quiet residential Hancock Street, are the
best bargains around at about $15 per person. You may have to
give up the luxury of a private bath, but rooms are clean and
downtown Bar Harbor is only a five-minute walk.

On Mt. Desert Street, also convenient to downtown, is a
whole string of inns. **The Ledgelawn Inn**, built in 1904, is a
Victorian-style inn that boasts modern comforts such as a
swimming pool, sauna, jacuzzi, and bar. Double rooms start at
$85 during the summer season and $55 in the off-season. The
inn is open from April through Thanksgiving (207-288-4596).
The Mira Monte Inn (207-288-4268), **Holbrook House**
(207-288-4970), and **Primrose Cottage Inn** (207-288-4031),

also on Mt. Desert Street, all offer comfortable lodging in attractive surroundings. A double room averages about $80 per night in any of these establishments, including a continental breakfast.

There are countless motels and cottages along Route 3 as you approach Bar Harbor from Ellsworth. If you're not planning to visit during the month of August or on a holiday weekend, you can probably check into any one of these without advance reservations. The Bar Harbor Chamber of Commerce will send you a useful brochure with detailed lodging listings free of charge. Write them at P.O. Box 158, Bar Harbor, ME 04609, or call (207) 288-5103 for your copy. If you plan to visit during the winter months, be sure to call ahead, as many businesses close at the end of October.

Northeast Harbor, only 12 miles farther on Route 3 from Bar Harbor, can be a welcome alternative to Bar Harbor's summer throngs and is equally convenient to Acadia. If your budget permits, the view of the harbor from the **Asticou** (207-276-3344) is first-rate and so is the service. It is best to book well in advance, particularly for August, and the oceanside rooms naturally fill up first. Double rooms start at $160 mid-June through mid-September and cost less than half that during the off-season. In the center of Northeast Harbor, the **Maison Suisse Inn** (207-276-5223) provides attractive guest rooms complete with four-poster beds and cozy down comforters to take the nip out of the Maine night air. The inn is open seasonally from May through October. Double rooms start at $80, and suites range from $125 to $155, breakfast included.

Camping
Blackwoods Campground, about eight miles from Bar Harbor and one mile from Seal Harbor off of Route 3, is the only campground in the heart of Acadia National Park. Several miles from the Seal Harbor entrance to Acadia, it is operated by the Park Service. The sites are more heavily wooded than in most private campgrounds in the area, and there's a path to the ocean. Reservations may be made through Ticketron outlets or by mail up to eight weeks in advance, and it is recommended that they be made at least three weeks in advance. It may be possible to obtain a site on your arrival on a space-available basis. Generally, the earlier in the day you arrive, the better chance of success you'll have. There are bathrooms on the premises and a shower nearby. For provisions, there is a small store in Seal Harbor, and you'll find more substantial offerings at the Pine Tree Market on Main Street in Northeast Harbor about four miles away. Write Acadia National Park, P.O. Box 177, Bar Harbor, ME 04609, for reservations.

A number of campgrounds are reasonably close to Bar Harbor on Route 3 between Bar Harbor and Ellsworth. **Bar Harbor Campground** (207-288-5185) is only 4½ miles from the center of town and three miles from the main entrance to Acadia. It has modern facilities, including a heated pool. **Mount Desert Narrows Camping Resort** (207-288-4782), eight miles from Bar Harbor, has RV hookups and ocean sites available. **Barcadia Campground** (207-288-3520) is about ten miles from Bar Harbor on the water.

Dining

No trip to the Maine seacoast is complete without a lobster dinner, and **Abel's Lobster Pound** on Route 198 in Somesville won't disappoint you. Abel's is open for dinner only. Reservations are recommended—call (207) 276-5827.

The Reading Room at the Bar Harbor Inn (207-288-3351) at the base of Main Street and **The Rinehart Dining Pavilion** (207-288-5663) on Eden Street in Bar Harbor both offer quality dining with arresting ocean views. While seafood dominates their menus, landlubbers will enjoy the Rinehart's prime rib. **George's** (207-288-4505), on Stephen's Lane behind the First National Bank building on Main Street, is not situated on the water, but its elegant ambience and unique presentation of traditional dishes warrant a visit. Dinner entrées start at about $15 at all three restaurants.

For more moderately priced meals, **Testa's** (207-288-3327) on Main Street has been a Bar Harbor institution for over 50 years, specializing in family-style Italian cuisine and seafood dishes. Dinner entrées start around $8. **Epi's** on Cottage Street uses only natural ingredients in their subs, pizzas, and pasta salads. Prices are inexpensive, and you can eat your meal in their casual booths or take it out. **Jordan's Restaurant**, farther down Cottage Street at number 80, is *the* spot to go for breakfast. Jordan's is known for the best "blues" on the island—meaning blueberry muffins. Their blueberry pancakes are also tasty. They do a brisk business, so service is fast and curt.

ACADIA NATIONAL PARK

Acadia National Park is the easternmost national park in the country. If you stand atop Cadillac Mountain at dawn, they say, you can be the first person in the United States to see the sunrise. The park, which encompasses rocky coastline, sheltered coves, wooded mountain trails, freshwater lakes, and ocean vistas, was donated by conservation-minded individuals, rather than being purchased outright by the government, to create a national park. Today you'll see why they felt the land should be preserved.

Suggested Schedule

9:00 a.m.	Start your day in Acadia at the visitor information center, then enter the park loop road.
1:00 p.m.	Picnic lunch on scenic Somme Sound.
3:30 p.m.	Enjoy tea on the lawn at the Jordan Pond Restaurant.
5:00 p.m.	Drive to the summit of Cadillac Mountain.
7:00 p.m.	Have a light dinner and stroll by Bar Harbor's many souvenir shops.

Travel Route

You'll drive about 50 miles before the day is over, all within the relatively small area of Mount Desert Island. Start the drive at Acadia's visitor information center, three miles west of Bar Harbor just off of Route 3. After leaving the visitor's center, take the Park Loop Road in the direction of Sand Beach.

After visiting the Wild Garden, Abbe Museum, Sand Beach, and Thunder Hole, exit the park road at Seal Harbor and drive three miles to Northeast Harbor on Route 3. From the center of Northeast Harbor, follow signs to Sargent Drive, which will take you by some of the harbor's more exclusive residences. Just past the Tennis Club, a turnout on your left offers a view overlooking Somme Sound, the only natural fiord on the East Coast. The spot is ideal for a picnic; just be sure to save room for afternoon tea.

If you're traveling by camper, motorcycle, or recreational vehicle, you'll need to retrace your steps at this point to the Stanley Brook entrance to Acadia (where you exited for Seal and Northeast harbors), as only automobiles are allowed on Sargent Drive, and traveling it on foot is impractical. By car, follow Sargent Drive along majestic Somme Sound until it intersects with

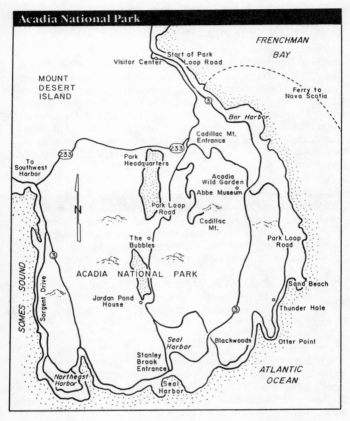

Acadia National Park

FRENCHMAN BAY

MOUNT DESERT ISLAND

Visitor Center
Start of Park Loop Road

Ferry to Nova Scotia

Bar Harbor

Cadillac Mt. Entrance

To Southwest Harbor

Park Headquarters

Acadia Wild Garden
Abbe Museum

Park Loop Road

Cadillac Mt.

The Bubbles

Park Loop Road

SOMES SOUND

ACADIA NATIONAL PARK

Sand Beach

Sargent Drive

Jordan Pond House

Thunder Hole

Seal Harbor

Blackwoods

Otter Point

Stanley Brook Entrance

Northeast Harbor

Seal Harbor

ATLANTIC OCEAN

Route 3. Take Route 3 back to Northeast Harbor and reenter
Park Loop Road at the Stanley Brook entrance.

Back on Park Loop Road, drive to Jordan Pond. From Jordan
Pond, continue on the park road to the turnoff for Cadillac
Mountain. After visiting the summit, return to Park Loop Road;
then exit onto Route 233 to return to Bar Harbor.

Sightseeing Highlights

▲▲▲ **Acadia National Park** covers over 35,000 acres. The
largest portion of the park, and the most visited by tourists, is
on Mount Desert Island, so named for its treeless top in the
early 1600s by French explorer Samuel de Champlain. Frenchman's Bay, whose name also derives from the French Colonial
era, lies between Mount Desert and the Schoodic Peninsula,

where there is an extension of Acadia. Entrance to the park costs $5 per car for a seven-day pass. Be sure to bring your binoculars, as seals and otters can often be seen playing on rocks just offshore.

The Visitor Information Center is a good place to familiarize yourself with the park. A 15-minute introductory film to Acadia is shown every half hour. Pick up a free map while you're here, along with a list of hiking trails if you wish to stray from the main road.

The **Wild Garden** is one of the first detours along the Park Loop. Plants you'll see throughout the park are labeled in this garden of wild flowers, making them easier to identify when you spot them in their natural habitat. The **Abbe Museum** at the same turnoff is a small museum of tools and artifacts used by the Indians who were the island's first settlers.

Back on the loop, you'll come to **Sand Beach**, unusual because most beaches you see on Mount Desert are rugged and rocky. Even on the hottest of summer days, this beach is kept cool by ocean breezes. The trail to **Great Head** starts at the far end of the beach. Further along the park road is **Thunder Hole**, where wave erosion has created a hole in the rocks which resounds with a booming noise as the waves crash to shore.

The restaurant at **Jordan Pond** serves a marvelous afternoon tea on the lawn with a splendid view of the pond and the "Bubbles"—two matching rounded mountains shaped by glaciers. If solitude is more your cup of tea, take a leisurely walk on the nature trail or on one of the flat paths alongside the pond. Find your own secluded rock and just soak up the scenery. The **Gate House** across the road from the restaurant is also worth a closer look because of its unique stone architecture.

The drive to **Cadillac Summit** will be the high point of your day both literally and figuratively, as it is the highest point on the Atlantic Coast. Though the climb by automobile takes about ten minutes without stopping, scores of breathtaking vistas will no doubt slow your progress. (The climb and descent will put a strain on your vehicle, so be sure to check the fluids and brakes before starting the ascent.) An arresting panorama awaits atop Cadillac Mountain. (Both the mountain and the luxury automobile were named after the same Frenchman.) From the summit one can see the harbors below, the Porcupine and Cranberry islands dotting the foreground, and Winter Harbor, Ironbound, and Schoodic across Frenchman's Bay. The view is particularly spectacular at sunrise and sunset, and the summit is also a popular stargazing post. The road is closed from midnight until one hour before sunrise.

Helpful Hints

Many people choose to see Acadia from a bicycle or moped seat rather than through a windshield. Except for the road to Cadillac Summit, which is demanding enough for a four-cylinder engine, two-wheel transportation is a refreshing way to explore the park. Rentals are available in downtown Bar Harbor. Mopeds from **Mopeds of Maine** on Main Street (288-4387) run $30 for the first two hours and $5 for each additional hour. Bicycles can be rented from **Acadia Bike & Canoe** at 48 Cottage Street (288-5483) for about $15 to $20 per day.

A sightseeing cruise on Frenchman's Bay is another agreeable way to survey the park and islands. **Frenchman's Bay Boating Company** next to the municipal pier in Bar Harbor offers a variety of cruising options. Call (207) 288-3322 for more information.

Just for Kids

About 12 miles west of Bar Harbor on Route 3, a three-mile stretch of highway has enough mini-golf courses, ice cream parlors, paddle boats, go-cart tracks, water slide parks—and even a small zoo—to bring just about any travel-weary child out of the doldrums.

Itinerary Options

Those with more time may wish to go on to Southwest and Bass harbors and the western part of Acadia from Northeast Harbor, rather than return to the main Park Loop Road immediately. From Bass Harbor you can take a ferry to Swan's Island, and another ferry operates from Northeast Harbor to the Cranberry Islands.

There are also over 120 miles of trails within Acadia to tempt the hiker. If you are so inclined and have the opportunity to stay a day or two longer, investigate some of them on your own.

The Schoodic Peninsula, directly across Frenchman's Bay from Bar Harbor, is also part of Acadia National Park. Because of its distance from the heart of Acadia, Schoodic is much less traveled but no less scenic. Take an extra day to traverse this more remote part of the park and the quiet fishing village of Winter Harbor. To get there, you'll need to take Route 3 back to Ellsworth and continue on US 1 North to West Gouldsboro. Then take Route 186 to Winter Harbor.

For those with lots of time on their hands, Nova Scotia is just a six-hour ferry ride away from Bar Harbor on the *Bluenose*. From mid-June through mid-September, the famous ferry departs daily for Yarmouth at 8:00 a.m. One-way passenger fare is $32.25 for adults, $16.10 for children ages 5 to 12. Automobiles and motor homes up to 20 feet cost $60 one-way. The ferry runs on a reduced schedule the rest of the year, and fares are lower. Call (800) 432-7344 or (207) 288-3397 for further information and reservations. Gambling is allowed on board once the ship reaches international waters. In Nova Scotia, the most scenic routes are along the province's coasts. The Cabot Trail on Cape Breton at the easternmost end of Nova Scotia is generally considered to the be the province's most beautiful region. From Caribou, Nova Scotia, you can take the ferry to sleepy Prince Edward Island, where deserted, white sand beaches meet a surprisingly warm, blue sea.

MT. WASHINGTON

The trip across Maine, approximately four hours from Bar Harbor to Bethel, is the longest stretch of straight driving without a stop on the entire trip. However, as you approach the White Mountains the views make the journey quite a pleasant one. The beauty of western Maine and New Hampshire's White Mountain National Forest is today's focal point.

Suggested Schedule

7:30 a.m.	Early breakfast at Jordan's.
8:30 a.m.	Leave Bar Harbor.
12:30 p.m.	Lunch in Bethel, Maine.
2:30 p.m.	Take the auto road to the top of Mt. Washington, the highest peak in the northeastern United States.
6:00 p.m.	Check into your accommodations.
7:00 p.m.	Dine in either Jackson or North Conway.

Travel Route: Bar Harbor to Mt. Washington (200 miles)
Take Route 3 West from Bar Harbor to Ellsworth. At Ellsworth follow US 1A toward Bangor. Just before Bangor, get onto Interstate 395 West, which will take you to US 2. Stay on US 2 all the way to Gorham, New Hampshire. In the center of Gorham, turn left onto Route 16 South. The entrance to the Mt. Washington Auto Road is about eight miles from Gorham on your right. After stopping at Mt. Washington, continue on Route 16 to Jackson or North Conway.

Sightseeing information is not the only reason to stop at the information center on Route 16 just outside North Conway in Intervale. The panorama of the Mt. Washington Valley from the parking lot is one of the finest around.

Sightseeing Highlights
▲▲▲ **Mt. Washington**—At 6,288 feet, this is the highest peak in the Northeast. On clear days, the panoramas from the ascent and summit are unrivaled. On top are a weather station and complete tourist facilities. Even in July the peak's climate can be quite brisk, so be sure to bring warm clothing with you. The summit can be reached by the auto road in your own vehicle at a cost of $10 for car and driver, plus $4 for each additional adult, $3 for each child ages 5 to 12. However, do not take those bumper stickers that read "This Car Climbed Mt. Washington"

lightly. The climb to the top is not easy, even for an automobile in top-notch condition. Should you prefer not to put the wear and tear on your vehicle, vans are available to take riders to the summit. They cost $14 per adult and $9 per child ages 5 to 12. After five hours on the road, you may find it a welcome relief to let a tour guide do the driving. There is also cog railway service from the other side of Mt. Washington at Bretton Woods. The round-trip by rail costs $27 and takes three hours.

Of course, many hikers try their luck at climbing the mountain. Should you wish to do so, you'll need a whole day. The information center across from the entrance to the auto road can suggest trails that are right for your ability. It is fairly easy for weary hikers to get rides back down the mountain from people who have taken the auto road. Camping shelters along the trail provide sanctuary for hikers who get caught in bad weather or just want to spend more time exploring the region.

▲ **Gondola Skyride**—For a different perspective on Mt. Washington, take the gondola at Wildcat Ski Area, which faces the mountain. The ride operates daily during July, August, and September from 10:00 a.m. to 4:30 p.m. and on weekends during June. Tickets are $6 for adults and $3 for children ages 6 to 12.

Jackson—About eight miles south of Wildcat is a covered bridge leading to the town of Jackson. Although Jackson does have Black Mountain, a downhill ski area, the town is best known as a cross-country skiers' haven. There are plenty of cozy bed and breakfasts around to take care of tired winter and summer visitors alike.

North Conway—Mt. Cranmore in nearby North Conway is one of the oldest ski areas in the Northeast. Although rail service is no longer available, trains used to arrive from Boston on a regular basis dropping skiers off right in the heart of the village. For this reason, the town has been catering to tourists for many years, and the effects are beginning to show. In the past ten years, factory outlets and the multitude of shoppers they bring have begun to crowd the town's charming core. Still, North Conway has its appeal, which includes the greatest variety of shops, restaurants, and lodging establishments in the Mt. Washington Valley.

▲ **Cathedral Ledge**—Just a few minutes from the center of North Conway, the ledge draws throngs of rock climbers and spectators alike. You'll probably find this daring sport fascinating to watch if you've never witnessed it firsthand. Climbers can be observed from below, or you can drive up the road to the top of the ledge and congratulate them as they reach their goal. Cool off after watching the climbers with a swim at neighboring Echo Lake State Park.

▲ **The Conway Scenic Railroad**—The railroad runs out of
North Conway's picturesque depot, which was built in 1874.
The train travels south along the Saco River, then crosses the
Swift River and Kancamagus Highway. Tickets for the one-hour
excursion, enjoyable to young and old alike, are $5 for adults
and $3 for children ages 4 to 12. Departure times are 11:00 a.m.,
1:00, 2:30, and 4:00 p.m. daily June through October. In July
and August there is also the Sunset Special which leaves on
selected nights at 7:00 p.m. Call (603) 356-5251 for information.

Mt. Washington Valley
There is plenty for children to do in the valley. **Storyland** on
Route 16 in Glen is a favorite of youngsters. Four miles west of
the junction of US 302 and Route 16, **Attitash Ski Area** in Bartlett operates an alpine slide and water park during the summer.
There is a mountain stream swimming hole at Jackson. Just follow the signs from Jackson center toward the Eagle Mountain
House. The swimming hole is about halfway up the hill on
your right.

Lodging
The **Eagle Mountain House** in Jackson is a charming resort on
a quiet country road with beautiful mountain views. The rooms
in the recently restored hotel are comfortably elegant and a rela-
tive bargain, starting at $80 in season and $60 during early
spring and late fall. Suites start at $120 during the summer and
$90 off-season. Tennis, golf, and swimming are all available at
the resort as well. Follow signs up Carter Notch Road from the
center of Jackson. Call (800) 527-5022 or (603) 383-9111 for
reservations.

The **Cranmore Inn**, only one block from the center of
North Conway on Kearsarge Street, is more reasonably priced
than many other inns in town yet offers the same services. A
comfortable room for two costs about $55 to $60 per night,
including an ample breakfast in a sunny breakfast room. There
are several sitting rooms and a swimming pool on the premises.
Mt. Cranmore Ski Area is only five minutes away. Call (603)
356-5502 for reservations.

Route 16 in North Conway is lined with inns and motels,
which can fill up at the height of the fall foliage season or for big
ski weekends. If you're calling ahead, try the **Scottish Lion**
(603-356-6381). The rooms are pleasant, meals are served with
a Scottish slant, and there is a lively pub to unwind in after a
long day of sightseeing or skiing. The inn also operates a Scottish import shop next door. The **White Trellis Motel** makes
more of an effort than most to create an attractive atmosphere

with flowering window boxes and fresh white paint (603-
356-2492).

Camping
Dolly Copp Campground is a national forest campground
near the base of Mt. Washington off Route 16, six miles south of
Gorham. The sites are assigned on a first-come, first-served
basis, as reservations are accepted for groups only. RVs are
allowed, but hot showers and electrical hook-ups are not available. Open from mid-May through mid-October.

    Glen Ellis Family Campground, on US 302 just west of the
Route 16 junction, is convenient to Jackson, North Conway, and
tomorrow's travel route. In case you're low on provisions, there
is a supermarket located next to the entrance, while the campground itself has complete sanitary and recreational facilities.
Some sites are adjacent to the Saco River. The campground
operates seasonally from Memorial Day to Columbus Day, July
being the busiest month. Call (603) 383-9320 for information in
season or (516) 746-2759 for inquiries during the winter.

Dining
The **Millbrook Tavern** at the Bethel Inn in Bethel, Maine, is a
good place to stop for lunch. The inn is open year-round, and
outdoor dining on the terrace is available during the summer
months. Lunch prices start at $5 for sandwiches. Those with
extra time and golf clubs or tennis rackets might choose to make
use of the inn's sports facilities. The inn is also an agreeable
home base should you wish to linger in the area. If you're traveling with your own provisions, there are plenty of picnic areas
along US 2 that are pleasant spots for an alfresco meal.

    For dinner, one can enjoy fine dining in Jackson at either the
Eagle Mountain House or the **Wentworth Hotel** (383-9700).
More moderately priced meals can be had at the **Thompson
House Eatery** right in the center of Jackson. Not too far from
Jackson, **The Bernerhof Inn** on US 302 West in Glen, just two
miles from the Route 16 intersection, serves appetizing Euro-
pean dishes with a German flair (383-4414).

    In North Conway, just across from the railroad depot on Main
Street, **Horsefeather's** menu ranges from deluxe burgers to
pasta and chicken entrées. The tavern atmosphere is lively, and
prices are moderate (356-2687). Also in North Conway's center
on Seavey Street one block up from Main Street, **Bellini's**
serves Italian specialties, including homemade pastas prepared
in delicious combinations. Try the fettucini with prosciutto,
spinach, and mushrooms in a light cream sauce. If you have
room, their desserts are also scrumptious. Dinner entrées start

at $8 (356-7000). For breakfast try the **Big Pickle Restaurant** next door to Bellini's on Seavey Street.

Itinerary Options
The Oxford Hills region of Maine near Bethel, with its beautiful freshwater lakes, such as Norway, Thompson, and Long, its mineral- and gem-rich landscape, and its numerous wooded trails, is a pleasant place for hikers, rockhounds, and fishermen to spend some extra time.

More adventurous travelers may find a river trip to their liking. Saco Bound in Conway, New Hampshire, operates a variety of river trips, including whitewater and flatwater, by raft or canoe for as little as several hours or up to several days. Contact them at (603) 447-2177 or Box 119, Center Conway, NH 03813, for more details.

WHITE MOUNTAIN NATIONAL FOREST

The White Mountain National Forest is a 750,000-acre expanse in central New Hampshire that encompasses much of the Presidential Mountain Range, including 6,288-foot Mt. Washington, as well as a bounty of alpine lakes, streams, cascades, and hiking trails. Today you'll explore this lush region before crossing the border into Vermont.

Suggested Schedule

8:00 a.m.	Breakfast.
9:00 a.m.	Spend the morning and early afternoon savoring the White Mountain National Forest's natural attractions. Enjoy a picnic lunch with an alpine backdrop.
2:00 p.m.	Leave the national forest and travel to Woodstock, Vermont, pausing along the way to visit a mine, a maple sugarhouse, a glassblowing exhibit, and an early farm museum; or hike to the bottom of a gorge.
6:00 p.m.	Check into lodging.
7:00 p.m.	Dinner.

Travel Route: Jackson/North Conway to Woodstock, Vermont (150 miles)
Route 16 South from Jackson or North from North Conway intersects with US 302 at Glen. Take US 302 West toward Bartlett and Twin Mountain. You will be passing through Crawford Notch State Park. At Twin Mountain, get onto US 3 South until it merges with Franconia Notch Parkway. Continue south on the parkway, exiting to see the forest's natural attractions. Exits are marked, and parking is provided.

After leaving Franconia Notch State Park, stay on US 3 South to Interstate 93 South. (Those with more time may want to remain on US 3 South and stop off at New Hampshire's largest lakes, Winnipesaukee and Squam.) The mountain views from I-93 are breathtaking. Exit I-93 at Route 104 West. At Danbury, proceed on US 4 West all the way to Woodstock, Vermont. Your total mileage for the day will be around 150 miles.

Alternate Route: From Lincoln just below the Flume, take Route 112 West to Route 118 South. At Warren, Route 188 merges

The White Mountains

with Route 25. Continue south to Wentworth. From Went-worth, follow Route 25A West to Fairlee. From Fairlee, travel on Route 10 South to Hanover, home of Dartmouth College, the Ivy League's northernmost member. After visiting Hanover, cross the Connecticut River to Norwich, Vermont. From Norwich, follow US 5 South to White River Junction, where you can pick up US 4 West to Woodstock. This alternate route enables you to see the lovely college town of Hanover but will not save you any time over the main travel route.

The popular Kancamagus Highway (Route 112) that runs west from Conway to Lincoln through the White Mountain National Forest is also a lovely route. However, I prefer the trip through Crawford and Franconia notches because the views are better and there is more to see along the way.

Crawford Notch State Park is in the heart of the White Mountain National Forest. As you travel through the park, you'll pass two small waterfalls, the Silver and Flume cascades, that slither, rather than plunge, down the mountainside. Both have parking areas. The better mountain view is from the Flume Cascade parking lot. The park's information center is located in a colorful train station near Twin Mountain.

As you approach Twin Mountain, there is a striking view of the Mt. Washington Hotel at Bretton Woods. Built in 1902, the hotel was designed to entice the jet set, and it still holds a commanding presence over the valley. In its heyday, visitors came by the trainload to visit the hotel. Today Bretton Woods is a thriving cross-country ski mecca. The entrance to the cog railway that climbs Mt. Washington is just beyond the hotel. The three-hour round-trip to the summit costs $27 for adults, $13.50 for youths ages 7 to 15; children under six years of age are free, and discounts are available for seniors. The train runs from late April through early November.

Cannon Mountain Ski Area is at the entrance to **Franconia Notch State Park**. Cannon operates a tramway during nonskiing months (adults $6.50, children ages 6 to 12 $3.50). While at Cannon, you can also visit the **New England Ski Museum** to learn more about the regional history of the sport through an audiovisual presentation. The museum is open from mid-May through mid-October and again just after Christmas for the winter ski season. A small admission fee is charged. The turnoff to **Old Man in the Mountain** is just after Cannon Mountain and **Echo Lake.** This portion of cliffs overlooking **Profile Lake** was so named because erosion has given the rocks the appearance of an old man from certain angles. You will see the old man's profile on many of New Hampshire's highway route signs.

Other highlights of the park include **the Basin** and **the Flume**. Swirling with water, the Basin is a natural pothole formed by ice-age glaciers and mountain cascades. There is wheelchair access to the Basin. Swimming is prohibited. A well-maintained bike path runs through this section of the park, and hiking trails abound. You may wish to hike one of the trails that leave from the Basin area, which are likely to be less crowded than the Flume trail. They are also free of charge.

The Flume is a narrow, moss-covered granite gorge. After hiking the Flume, you can return to the visitor's center or continue on the trail to view a waterfall and natural pool. Plan to spend about an hour and a half if you decide to hike the entire loop. Although there are buses that can take you from the visitor's center halfway to the Flume, much of the arduous walking still lies ahead. There is no handicapped access to the Flume. There is an admission charge of $5 for adults, $2.50 for children ages 6 to 12. The trail is refreshingly cool on hot summer days, but on brisk autumn days you may want to bring an extra sweater or jacket along. The Flume is open from 9:00 a.m. to 4:30 p.m. daily June through October.

Rock collectors will want to stop at **Ruggles Mine** near Grafton, off US 4 between Interstate 93 and White River Junction. The mine first opened in 1803 and is known for its vast supply of mica. Visitors are allowed to take home mineral samples they collect. The mine is open on weekends only from mid-May through mid-June, daily mid-June through mid-October from 9:00 a.m. to 5:00 p.m., until 6:00 p.m. during July and August. Admission is $5.50 for adults and $2.50 for children ages 6 to 11.

Just after you pass into Quechee, Vermont, on US 4, only a few miles from the Vermont/New Hampshire state line, there is an information booth on your left. Several hundred yards beyond that, a bridge crosses the dramatic Queeche Gorge. The depth of the gorge at the bridge is 165 feet. Parking is available on both sides of the bridge. Take the one-mile hike to the bottom of the gorge or just stretch your legs on the short (¼-mile) hike to view the waterfall that empties into the river below.

A right-hand turn at the first blinking light after the gorge bridge will take you through one of New England's rustic covered bridges and into "downtown" Quechee. There, Simon Pearce has completely renovated the old mill, so today you can watch glassblowers and potters performing their crafts. You can also inspect the modern hydraulic power system that now fuels the ovens. The handmade glassware and pottery is sold in the gift shop along with natural fiber fabrics. The shop is open from 10:00 a.m. to 5:00 p.m., and you can watch glassblowing during the same hours, except from 1:00 p.m. to 2:00 p.m. when the craftsmen take their lunch break. Admission is free.

From Simon Pearce, continue on River Road for several miles past lush green golf courses and farms. Should you wish to visit a maple sugarhouse to learn about processing the sweet syrup, turn onto Hillside Road and follow signs to Sugarbush Farm. Although sugaring season is in the spring, the farm is open year-round and also makes tasty Vermont cheeses. Call (802) 457-1757 for hours of operation during your visit. Should you visit Sugarbush Farm, return to River Road and cross the Taftsville Covered Bridge which will take you back onto US 4. Woodstock is only three miles from here.

Woodstock appears to be the kind of place that crime or hardship never touches, a model New England town with elegant Federal-style homes surrounding a town green where every blade of grass seems perfectly groomed. A tourist information booth right on the town green will answer questions. The booth is open from 10:00 a.m. to 6:00 p.m. The Town Crier Chalk Board in the center of the business district lists the goings-on for the day.

The **Billings Farm and Museum** is off Route 12 north of Woodstock. The farm offers a look at rural Vermont life of a century ago. You can help hand-churn butter, see how cows were

milked the old-fashioned way, and watch woodcarving demonstrations. The farm is open daily May through October from
10:00 a.m. to 5:00 p.m. Admission is charged.

Lodging

For those who want the comfort of a country inn combined
with resort amenities such as golf, tennis, and swimming, the
Woodstock Inn & Resort right on the town green is the place
to stay. Double rooms start at $100 per night. Call (802)
457-1100 for reservations.

At the **Woodstock House Bed & Breakfast** on the west
side of town, a night's lodging, including breakfast the next
morning, will run about $60 for two (802-457-1758). **The Lin-
coln Covered Bridge Inn** on US 4 in nearby West Woodstock
overlooks the Lincoln Covered Bridge and the Ottauquechee
River. Special touches include herb potpourri in the guest
rooms and homemade breads and muffins for continental
breakfast. Double room rates run from $75 to $95. There is also
a restaurant on the premises. Call (802) 457-3312 for reservations. The **Braeside Motel** on the east side of Woodstock
offers accommodations at moderate prices (802-457-1366), and
Rutland about 40 minutes farther along US 4 West has a much
wider selection of reasonably priced lodging establishments.

Camping

The closest camping area to Woodstock is the state-operated
Quechee Recreation Area near the Quechee Gorge. A trail
runs from the camping area to the bottom of the gorge. Both
tent and camper sites are available. For information call (802)
295-2990 or write Vermont Forest Parks & Recreation at 363
River Street, North Springfield, VT 05450.

Dining

Bentley's Restaurant in Woodstock Center serves dishes ranging from veal to Szechuan to fresh salads. Dinner entrées are
priced from $14 to $18. Families may want to try **Spooner's
Restaurant** in Spooner Barn on US 4 just east of Woodstock
Center. Spooner's has a children's menu, and specialties include
western-style beef and traditional New England fare (802-457-
4022). Prices are moderate.

For elegant dining, **The Prince and the Pauper** on Elm
Street in Woodstock might even please royalty. The prix fixe
menu at $25 per person includes items such as poached salmon
and roast duckling. Call (802) 457-1818.

The **Downtown Deli** serves breakfast daily from 7:00 a.m. if
breakfast is not included with your lodging.

SOUTHERN VERMONT

This area of New England is particularly well traveled in autumn because of the abundant maple trees that turn brilliant orange and red as they begin producing their sweet sap. Southern Vermont's excellent ski resorts, beautiful mountain vistas, and charming towns with their tidy village greens are reason enough to visit the region in any season.

Suggested Schedule

9:00 a.m.	Leave Woodstock for Manchester. Visit the Vermont Marble Exhibit or Wilson Castle in Proctor on the way.
11:30 a.m.	Window shop in Manchester Center and stroll along lovely Manchester Village's marble sidewalks.
1:00 p.m.	Lunch.
2:00 p.m.	Visit Hildene.
3:30 p.m.	Take the Sky Line Drive to the top of Mt. Equinox, or if the weather refuses to cooperate, take your pick of the area's many other attractions.
5:00 p.m.	Check into a country inn for a memorable evening of fine dining and provincial comfort.

Travel Route: Woodstock to Manchester (64 miles)

From Woodstock, take US 4 to Rutland, passing by Killington and Pico ski areas. US 4 connects with US 7 at Rutland. To travel to Proctor, continue on US 4 to Route 3 North. Then backtrack to the junction of US 4 and US 7 and take US 7 South from Rutland to Manchester Center. All along US 7 there are views of the Green Mountains on your left. Historic Manchester Village is one mile from Manchester Center on Route 7A.

Manchester Center has an array of tidy shops interspersed with outlets such as Ralph Lauren and Benetton. The Northshire Bookstore at the intersection of US 7 and Route 11/30 is worth a visit, as is Hand Works on the Green, a contemporary crafts gallery opposite the Chamber of Commerce. Orvis, the mail order giant, has its flagship store on Route 7A in Manchester.

The Chamber of Commerce, located on the main green as you enter Manchester Center on US 7 traveling south, is very helpful with sightseeing information. They're open from 9:00

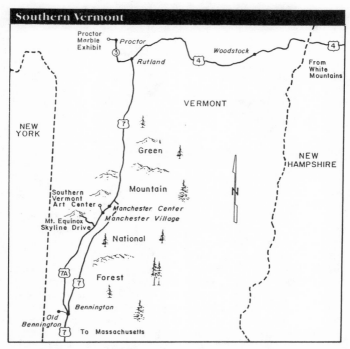

Southern Vermont

a.m. to 5:00 p.m. during the week and from 10:00 a.m. to 4:00 p.m. on weekends. Hikers will want to stop in at the U.S. Forest Service office in Manchester on Route 11/30 for local hiking suggestions. Skiers will be pleased to know that both Stratton and Bromley mountains are convenient to the Manchester area.

Sightseeing Highlights

▲ **Vermont Marble Exhibit**—Proctor, a town about eight miles from Rutland, calls itself the "marble capital of the world" because of the abundance of marble found in this area. At the Vermont Marble Exhibit on Main Street, visitors have the chance to see a marble sculptor at work. A film explains the natural forces that created marble and the steps man takes to shape the stone for his purposes. You will see examples of Vermont marble throughout Proctor and, later in the day, in Manchester Village. The marble exhibit is open daily mid-May through late October from 9:00 a.m. to 5:30 p.m. Winter hours are Monday through Saturday 9:00 a.m. to 4:00 p.m. Admission is charged.

▲ **Wilson Castle** —On West Proctor Road off US 4, west of

Rutland about one-half mile from the Route 3 North turnoff, this nineteenth-century castle is filled with both European and Oriental furnishings and has scores of stained-glass windows. There is also an aviary on the 115-acre estate. The castle is open daily for guided tours during the summer. Admission is charged. Children under six are free. Call (802) 773-3284 for hours during your visit.

▲ **Southern Vermont Art Center**—The center is only open from June through mid-October. After viewing the changing exhibits by local artists, take a walk in the sculpture garden, on the botany trail, or have lunch in the attractive garden café, which has a different menu daily. Lunch entrées are in the $8 range. Adult admission to the center is $3. To get to the center, follow signs from Route 7A in Manchester.

▲▲ **Hildene**—This Georgian revival mansion just south of Manchester Village on Route 7A was owned by Robert Todd Lincoln, son of Abraham Lincoln. Hildene remained in the Lincoln family until 1975 and is now open to the public. The furnishings, including a player pipe organ, belonged to the Lincolns. There are formal gardens on the estate, as well as an area called the Meadowlands where many special events such as polo, symphony concerts, sleigh rides, and cross-country skiing take place. Even though the home is only open for tours from mid-May through October, you many want to call (802) 362-1788 to see if there are any special goings-on should your visit happen to fall in the off-season. Admission to the house is $5 for adults, $2 for children, and the last tour of the day leaves at 4:00 p.m.

▲ **Norman Rockwell Exhibition and Gift Shop**—More a gift shop than a museum, this place on Route 7A in Arlington has hundreds of Rockwell magazine covers on display but no original work. There is a film presentation on Rockwell. Admission is $1, and the shop is open daily from 9:00 a.m. to 7:00 p.m. I prefer the Rockwell Museum in Stockbridge, Massachusetts, which you can visit two days later.

▲ **Sky Line Drive**—For better views of the Green Mountains, take the five-mile-long Sky Line Drive to the top of Mt. Equinox, the highest peak in the Taconic range. The drive is well worth taking on a clear day and is particularly dramatic at the height of fall foliage. There are numerous places to picnic or hike along the way. The toll is $5 per car, and the drive is open from 8:00 a.m. to 10:00 p.m. daily May through October. Entrance to the auto road is on Route 7A just south of Manchester Village.

Lodging
The majestic **Equinox Hotel** reigns supremely over historic Manchester Village. The eighteenth-century hotel has recently

been renovated and now serves as a 175-room resort. The grand exterior appears to stretch endlessly, as do the marble sidewalks that surround the building. Carriage rides are available from the hotel's doorstep. The hotel restaurant serves unusual dishes, such as salmon with a black bean and ginger sauce and veal with citrus fruits and apple hazelnut butter. Call (802) 362-4700 or (800) 362-4747 for reservations. Rooms in season will run over $120 per night for two.

The Reluctant Panther on West Road in Manchester Village (802-362-2568) has pleasing lodging and dining facilities, as does the lovely Victorian **Arlington Inn** on Route 7A in the center of nearby Arlington (802-375-6532). **The Inn at Manchester** on Route 7A in Manchester Village is open all year and serves a complete breakfast. Call (802) 362-1793 for reservations. Accommodations for two people at any of the three inns start around at least $80 nightly in season. For double occupancy rooms that run $50 a night and under, try the **Valhalla Motel** on Route 7A in Arlington. You can make reservations by calling the area lodging service at (802) 824-6915 which can help you find other accommodations in all price ranges.

Reservations for the Manchester area are strongly advised, especially on weekends and during leaf-peeping season. At the Equinox, for example, rooms are often completely booked as much as six months in advance for peak foliage weekends.

Camping
Emerald Lake State Park, in East Dorset about eight miles north of Manchester Center on US 7, has camping, swimming, a nature trail, and boating on a beautiful, green lake that lives up to its name. The camping area has 105 sites, no hook-ups, 35 lean-tos, bathrooms, and pay showers. Canoes and rowboats can be rented for an outing on the lake. Call (802) 362-1655 for reservations.

Camping on the Battenkill is a private campground with both tent and RV sites plus swimming and fishing on the Battenkill River. The campground, located on Route 7A in Arlington, is open from mid-April through October. Call (802) 375-6663 for rates.

Dining
For breakfast try **Up For Breakfast** on Main Street in Manchester Center, where specialties include huevos rancheros, eggs benedict, and chicken fritata. Or indulge in pancakes at the Pancake House on the south side of town. The **Park Bench**, also on the south side of town, is a popular lunch spot, or try either **Angelo's** (802-362-2408) Italian dishes or moderately priced basic American cuisine at **Quality Restaurant** in the

center of town. For dessert, the aroma from the **Cookie House** is hard to resist. Many of the local inns also have excellent restaurants.

If you want to ship home some of Vermont's celebrated cheddar cheese, the Grand Union supermarket in Manchester Center is one of the best places in the area to purchase it. They have the cheese already packed for shipping, and their prices tend to be lower than elsewhere. The Grand Union is also a good place to purchase Vermont maple syrup and prepared salads for picnicking.

Nightlife
During June, July, and August, one can enjoy summer stock productions at the **Dorset Playhouse** on Route 30 five miles north of Manchester Center. Call (802) 867-5777 for ticket information.

Itinerary Options
The Battenkill River, which runs from Manchester southwest through Arlington, is frequented by canoeists. **Battenkill Canoe, Ltd.** on Route 313 in West Arlington can outfit you with the canoe trip of your choice. Contact them at (802) 375-9559 for additional information.

Lake George, New York, a very popular lake resort, is only 43 miles from Rutland. To get to Lake George, continue on US 4 West from Rutland to Fort Ann. At Fort Ann take Route 149 West to US 9. Follow US 9 North to the town of Lake George.

Fort Ticonderoga, about 50 miles northwest of Rutland at Ticonderoga, New York, is also a favorite tourist destination. To get to the fort, continue on US 4 West at Rutland to Whitehall, then take Route 22 North to Ticonderoga.

An excursion I highly recommend for those with extra time is traveling 55 miles north from Rutland on US 7 to the town of Shelburne and the Shelburne Museum and Heritage Park. The Shelburne Museum is generally considered to have one of the best collections of Early American antiques and folk art. The museum is open daily from 9:00 a.m. to 5:00 p.m. from mid-May through mid-October. Admission is charged.

From Shelburne, it is just a hop, skip, and a jump to the thriving city of Burlington, Vermont, on beautiful Lake Champlain. A ferry ride across the lake can take you into Adirondacks country, and once across the lake, Montreal, Canada, is only a hundred-mile drive north on Interstate 87 (Canadian 15 once you cross the border).

BENNINGTON AND THE BERKSHIRES

Bennington, Vermont, was the site of a major revolutionary war victory for the colonists in 1777. Today, looking at Old Bennington's graceful homes, it is hard to believe that a war ever took place there.

Suggested Schedule

8:00 a.m.	Breakfast.
9:00 a.m.	Travel to Bennington and visit the Bennington Monument and Bennington Museum.
12:00 p.m.	Leave for Williamstown, Massachusetts.
12:30 p.m.	Lunch in Williamstown.
1:30 p.m.	Spend the afternoon exploring the Clark Institute and the Williams College art museum.
6:00 p.m.	Check into your Berkshire accommodation, which will be your home base for the next two nights.

Travel Route: Manchester to Stockbridge/Lenox (75 miles)

From the Manchester area, continue on Route 7A South to Bennington. Covered bridge enthusiasts should make a short detour at Arlington onto Route 313, where there are covered bridges on both sides of Route 7A. Farther along Route 7A, take Route 67 West at South Shaftsbury to Route 67A in North Bennington. There are two more covered bridges in quick succession along Route 67A as you approach Old Bennington.

Within Bennington itself, driving is confusing because roads are not well marked and route signs seem to contradict one another. The easiest way to get your bearings is to look for the Bennington Monument, which stands high on the hill above the town, and drive toward it. At the monument ask directions to the museum.

Leaving Bennington, take US 7 South, stopping in Williamstown for the afternoon, then continuing on US 7 to Lenox and Stockbridge in the heart of the Berkshire region.

Bennington Sightseeing Highlights

▲▲ **The Bennington Museum**—The primary reason for visiting this museum approximately one-half mile from the Bennington Monument on Route 9 is its collection of works by famed American folk artist Grandma Moses, who continued to

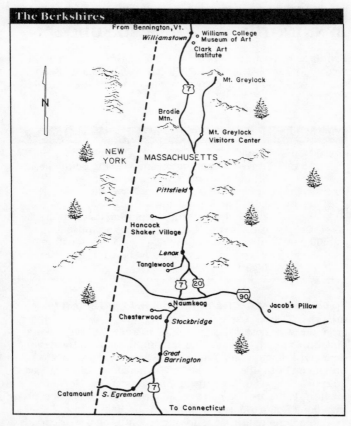

be productive well into her nineties. The museum's collection also includes Early American furniture, glassware, pottery, military artifacts, and household items such as pedal-operated sewing machines. The museum is open daily from 9:00 a.m. to 5:00 p.m. March through November. Admission is $4 for adults, $3 for students and senior citizens; children under 12, free. Family admission for two adults and two children under 18 is $10.

▲ **The Bennington Monument**—Completed in 1891, the monument commemorates the Battle of Bennington and is the centerpiece of lovely Old Bennington. It warrants a visit on any clear day for the view and is a must at the height of fall foliage season. You can see three states—Massachusetts, New York, and Vermont—from the observation deck. The well-groomed houses that line the road leading to and from the monument are worth a look as well. Admission to the monument is only $.50 for adults, $.25 for children. An elevator takes you to the top of the 306-foot structure, so there is no stair-climbing involved.

▲ **The Old First Church**—Adjacent to the town green in Old Bennington, this is a lovely example of early nineteenth-century church architecture in New England. Perhaps more interesting, though, is its graveyard with headstones dating back to the revolutionary war. Poet Robert Frost is buried here.

Williamstown Sightseeing Highlights

In this quintessential college town, Williams College dominates just about every aspect of town life, providing the residents of this sleepy Berkshire community with a wealth of cultural activities that many rural communities lack, including two outstanding art museums.

▲▲▲ **Sterling and Francine Clark Art Institute**—The museum has room after room of stunning French Impressionist paintings by Renoir and Monet, among others, and works by noted American painters such as Homer, Cassatt, and Sargent. The museum's fine collection also includes English silver and works dating back to the fifteenth century. Admission is free. Open 10.00 a.m. to 5:00 p.m. Tuesday through Sunday. Closed on Thanksgiving, Christmas, and New Year's Day.

▲▲ **Williams College Art Museum**—The museum's collection ranges from ancient Greek vases to Andy Warhol pop art. There is also a gallery devoted to Maurice and Charles Prendergast. No admission is charged. Open Monday through Saturday 10:00 a.m. to 5:00 p.m., Sundays from 1:00 p.m. to 5:00 p.m. The museum is closed for Thanksgiving, Christmas, and New Year's Day.

▲ **The Williamstown Theatre Festival**—The festival is widely known for its high-quality summer productions. Many popular actors got their start here, and some return on occasion to hone their stage skills. Call (413) 597-3400 for performance and ticket information.

Lodging

You can find comfortable lodging at the **Williams Inn** (413-458-9371) on the green in Williamstown if you plan to stay for a performance at the playhouse. If you're not attending the theater, I suggest putting up for the next two nights in Stockbridge or Lenox, both better jumping-off points for Berkshire activities.

The **Red Lion Inn** in Stockbridge is the best-known inn in the area and deservedly so. The Red Lion has been treating its guests regally for over 200 years and serves as the focal point of the town. If you are unable to book a room here, at least partake in a traditional New England meal in the main dining room or people-watch while sipping cocktails on the inn's front porch. Double rooms start around $80 in peak season (May through October). Singles and two-room suites are also available. Call (413) 298-5545 for reservations.

The Roy's Guesthouse is conveniently located in the center of Stockbridge directly across from the Old Corner House. There are no private baths, but rooms are air-conditioned in summertime. Rooms are about $50 to $70 in late spring and early fall and start at $65 during the summer (413-298-3448).

The attractively furnished **Berkshire Thistle Inn** is one block from the Red Lion on Pine Street. Reservations can be made by calling (413) 298-3188. Double rooms with queen-size beds start at $75 midweek in the off-season and $100 midweek July through October.

There is a whole strip of motels on US 7 between Pittsfield and Lenox. More motels can also be found on US 7 between Stockbridge and Great Barrington. The area abounds with country inns, but accommodations fill up quickly on weekends so you may want to call the Berkshire Visitor's Bureau at (413) 443-9186 for a complete lodging list.

Camping

The **Pittsfield State Forest** (413-442-8992) has 31 campsites and **October Mountain State Forest** (413-243-1778) in Lee has 50. The campground at October Mountain is more convenient to sights, so reservations are strongly recommended. Sites are about $6 per night. Both campgrounds have bathrooms with wheelchair access and are open seasonally. **Bonnie Brae Cabins and Campsites** at Pontoosuc Lake, just off US 7 several miles north of downtown Pittsfield, might also be an economical alternative to staying in a country inn. Open May through October, Bonnie Brae has cabins that rent for $45 per night as well as campsites. Call (413) 442-3754 for information.

Dining

For fine dining, try the Red Lion's prime rib, stuffed lobster, or scrod. Dinner entrées range from $15 to $25. The **Federal House** in South Lee, just about a mile and a half from Stockbridge, serves continental cuisine, and entrées start at $17. Call (413) 243-1824 for reservations. Somewhat less formal, **Michael's** on Elm Street in Stockbridge serves a variety of American dishes, with dinner prices ranging from $7 to $16. For gourmet take-out or eat-in pasta salads, try **La Fete Chez Vous** down an alley off Main Street between the Red Lion and Elm

Street. The **Cafe in the Mews** behind the Red Lion also serves salads and sandwiches for about $5.

Itinerary Options

If you'd prefer to spend your day outdoors, take the scenic drive over Mt. Greylock. On fair days the view of the Berkshires is extraordinary. The entrance to the visitor's center is off US 7 just south of New Ashford.

Horse racing fans traveling this route in August may want to take a 35-mile detour from Arlington, Vermont, to Saratoga Springs, New York. In addition to being recognized for thoroughbred horse racing and natural springs, Saratoga also has fine homes in its favor. The New York State Fair is held annually in Saratoga.

Deerfield, about 35 miles southeast of Williamstown, Massachusetts, is one of the most perfectly preserved historic towns in New England. While the majority of buildings are privately owned by either individuals or Deerfield Academy, some are open to the public. To get to Deerfield, take Route 2 East from Williamstown to Greenfield. From Greenfield, follow US 5 South to Deerfield.

THE BERKSHIRES

Because the Berkshires offer the visitor so much in the way of outdoor recreation, such as golf, skiing, and hiking, cultural events such as the Boston Symphony Orchestra at Tanglewood, picturesque villages such as Stockbridge, and, of course, the beauty of the Berkshire Hills themselves, the area has been a popular resort for over a hundred years. Couple the attractions with the fact that the Berkshires are only three hours from both New York City and Boston, and it is amazing that the area is not overrun with souvenir shop malls, factory outlets, and T-shirt shops designed to take advantage of the tourist dollar. Fortunately, due to careful planning, most towns remain much as they were when Norman Rockwell painted here in the 1950s, and many have changed little in the last century.

Suggested Schedule

9:00 a.m.	Breakfast.
10:00 a.m.	Visit Hancock Shaker Village.
12:30 p.m.	Lunch.
1:30 p.m.	Tour Chesterwood.
3:30 p.m.	Visit the Norman Rockwell Museum.
4:30 p.m.	Stroll down Main Street in Stockbridge, perhaps stopping at the Red Lion for tea or a cocktail and people-watching.
6:00 p.m.	Dinner.
8:00 p.m.	Take in an evening performance of the entertainment of your choice.

Travel Route
Travel to Hancock Shaker Village at the junction of US 20 and Route 41 about 12 miles northwest of Stockbridge. From the village, take Route 41 South to Route 102 East. Follow Route 102 East until it intersects with Route 183 South. Take Route 183 South and follow signs to Chesterwood. After leaving Chesterwood, retrace your steps back to Route 102 and continue on Route 102 East for two miles into the center of Stockbridge. The tourist information booth on Main Street in Stockbridge can provide you with directions to other points of interest in the area, and in most cases sights are well marked by directional signs.

Sightseeing Highlights

▲▲▲ **Hancock Shaker Village**—Allow at least two hours to explore this village, one of the best examples of the everyday life of an unusual religious sect called the Shakers. There are live demonstrations of Shaker crafts, such as broom making and basket weaving. Two 60-minute tours daily at 10:30 a.m. and 2:00 p.m. take you through part of the village. If you are unable to time your visit for a guided tour, you are free to tour the complex on your own. The descriptive panels in each room describe different aspects of Shaker life. Don't miss the unique round barn. The village is open daily from 9:30 a.m. to 5:00 p.m. May through October. The food concession at the visitor's center is surprisingly good—try the Mediterranean torte. The village is located at the junction of Routes 41 and 20 in Hancock. There are picnic tables outside the visitor center. Entrance fees are $7 for adults or $17 per family for those traveling with kids. Student and senior citizen admission is $6.25, and tickets for children ages 6 to 12 are $3 each.

▲ **The Berkshire Garden Center**—This 15-acre botanic garden off Route 102, just before you come to the intersection of Route 183, is a nice spot for a picnic lunch between visits to Hancock Shaker Village and Chesterwood. The center is open daily from 10:00 a.m. to 5:00 p.m. The greenhouses are open year-round, while the gardens are open May through October, and admission is charged during those months. Admission is $3 for adults, $2 for seniors, $.50 for children ages 6 to 12.

▲▲ **Chesterwood**—This was the summer home of sculptor Daniel Chester French, who is known for the Lincoln Memorial in Washington, D.C., and the Minute Man statue in Concord, Massachusetts, as well as many other works that adorn governmental buildings. Plaster castings of his works are displayed in his barn, home, and studio. Many of his works were so large he had to transport them out of his studio on railroad tracks just to see how they'd look in the sunlight. Usually beginning on July 4th weekend, contemporary sculpture from local artists is on exhibit each summer throughout the grounds and along the nature trail. Chesterwood is operated by the National Trust and is open daily May through October from 10:00 a.m. to 5:00 p.m. There is a picnic area next to the parking lot. Admission is $4 for adults.

▲▲ **The Norman Rockwell Museum**—This museum is currently housed in the Old Corner House on Main Street, with plans for a larger facility in the near future. Rockwell fans will enjoy this small, but choice, collection. Those previously indifferent to Rockwell will become converts when they witness the clarity and vitality of his oils firsthand. Open daily from 10:00 a.m. to 5:00 p.m., except for the last two weeks in January when the museum is closed. Admission is $4 for adults and $1 for children ages 5 to 18.

▲ **Naumkeag**—Designed by Stanford White, this stately home open to the public is about one-half mile from the Red Lion Inn on Prospect Hill Road. The formal gardens are open from 10:00 a.m. to 5:00 p.m. during the summer. The house may be toured Tuesday through Sunday beginning at 10:00 a.m., with the last tour leaving at 4:15 p.m. Admission to the house and gardens is $4.50, admission to the house alone is $3.50, and garden admission only is $2.50. Open seasonally.

▲ **The Mount**—Off US 7 between Lenox and Stockbridge, this was the summer estate of American novelist Edith Wharton. Perhaps her most famous novel, *Ethan Frome*, was set in Lenox. Although it is presently undergoing restoration, one can tour the property during the summer months. Admission is $3.50. Plays based on the author's works are presented here during July and August. Tickets to the matinee performances cost $15, which includes afternoon tea. Call (413) 637-1899 for complete details.

▲ **Arrowhead**—Author Herman Melville made his home here for thirteen years during the mid-1800s. See the room where Melville penned *Moby Dick* and several other novels. Located on Holmes Road in Pittsfield, Arrowhead is open for guided tours Memorial Day through October. Call (413) 442-1793 for hours. Admission is $3 for adults, $2.50 for seniors, $1.50 for youths ages 6 to 16.

Dining

If the dining possibilities in the Stockbridge/Lenox area are a little too pricey for your tastes, you may want to try those in Great Barrington, seven miles south of Stockbridge on US 7. Just off Main Street in the center of Great Barrington, three restaurants, all on Railroad Street, serve appetizing meals that won't deplete your pocketbook. **20 Railroad Street** (413-528-9345) offers basic tavern-style fare in a comfortable atmosphere. **Leona's & Violette's** just up the street serves falafel, shish-kabob, and other Lebanese dishes. Nearby, **Noodle's** is a little more expensive than the other two but still reasonable by Berkshire standards.

Just a few miles beyond Great Barrington, the town of South Egremont has a number of inns and restaurants, most notably the **Egremont Inn** on Old Sheffield Road, which is a respectable alternative to the Red Lion for both lodging and fine dining. Call (413) 528-2414 for reservations.

Nightlife
A visit to **Tanglewood**, the Boston Symphony Orchestra's summer home in Lenox, is the favorite form of nighttime entertainment in the Berkshires. The BSO performs in the "Shed" on lovely wooded grounds. Tickets are available for seating in the Shed, but on clear nights Beethoven is best heard with a champagne picnic on the lawn. Bring your own blanket and dress warmly. Early birds can catch afternoon rehearsal performances at bargain prices. Call the box office at (413) 637-1940 for information during the summer months. In the off-season, you'll need to contact the BSO's office in Boston, (617) 266-1492, for details. Tanglewood is located off Route 183 about two miles south of Lenox Center.

Jacob's Pillow is also a popular summer cultural event. The dance festival features various well-known and talented traveling dance troupes. The Pillow is located in Becket on US 20 about eight miles from Lee. Call (413) 243-0745 for schedule and tickets.

Other cultural events in the area include the **Berkshire Theatre Festival** in Stockbridge (413-298-5576), the **Berkshire Ballet** in Pittsfield (413-442-1307), the **Berkshire Opera Company** (413-243-1343), and **Stockbridge Chamber Concerts** at Seven Hills (413-637-0060).

Itinerary Option
From the Berkshires, it is only a two-hour drive to the Catskill Mountains in New York state. The Catskills are somewhat less traveled during fall foliage season than most of New England, but the scenery is no less spectacular. To get there, follow US 7 South to Great Barrington. From Great Barrington, follow Route 23 West to Hudson, New York. At Hudson, cross the Rip Van Winkle Bridge to Catskill, New York.

CONNECTICUT RIVER VALLEY

Leaving the Berkshires behind, you'll be exposed to a castle, a capital, and culture as you travel along the Connecticut River today.

Suggested Schedule

8:00 a.m.	Have breakfast and leave the Berkshires.
10:30 a.m.	Tour Nook Farm.
12:30 p.m.	Lunch in Hartford or picnic along the Connecticut River.
2:30 p.m.	Visit Gillette's Castle.
4:00 p.m.	Amble along Essex's Main Street.
5:00 p.m.	Have an early dinner or late afternoon snack at the Griswold Inn.
6:00 p.m.	Head on up the coast to settle in for the night in Mystic.

Travel Route: Stockbridge to Mystic (110 miles)
From Stockbridge, head south on US 7 through the antique-lovers' havens of South Egremont and Sheffield. At Canaan, take US 44 East. After entering West Hartford, turn right onto Prospect. In about five minutes you will come to the Farmington Avenue intersection; take a left onto Farmington. The parking lot for the Stowe and Twain houses is on your right immediately after the Woodland Street stoplight.

Alternative Route to Hartford: If you have extra time, a more scenic route from the Berkshires to Hartford is to travel through the northwestern corner of Connecticut, which many consider the prettiest part of the state. Instead of turning east at Canaan, continue on US 7 South to Kent, passing through West Cornwall, where there is a covered bridge. From Kent, take Route 341 East through Warren to Woodville. At Woodville, go east on US 202 to Litchfield, a showplace for exquisite eighteenth-century estates. The Congregational Church on Litchfield's village green is widely noted for its classic New England architecture. Leaving Litchfield, take Route 118 East to Route 4, then follow 4 East to West Hartford. Art lovers following this alternate route should visit the Hill-Stead Museum in Farmington, originally designed as a private home by architect Stanford White. The house is now filled with choice furnishings and impressionist paintings. Call (203) 677-4787 for hours and admission charges.

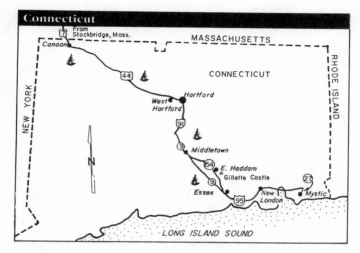

From Hartford, take Interstate 84 East to Interstate 91 South. Exit I-91 South at Route 9 South and pass by Middletown, home of Wesleyan University. At Exit 10 get onto Route 154 South. A good place to picnic is Haddam Meadows State Park, along the river just off Route 154. To visit the Goodspeed Opera House and Gillette's Castle, get onto Route 82 East and follow signs to both.

After conquering the castle, retrace your steps to Route 154 South and stay on it to Essex. Essex is an attractive town whose past and present have been shaped by nautical endeavors. In 1814, during the War of 1812, the British raided Essex and burned many of the town's ships, causing great hardship to the townspeople. Today, well-kept houses are discreetly tucked away on the waterfront, while the marina is filled with pleasure craft. From Essex, take Route 154 South until it intersects with Route 9. Take Route 9 South to Interstate 95 North and get off at the Mystic Exit, #90, Route 27.

Sightseeing Highlights

▲▲▲ **Nook Farm**—only a handful of houses remain from this nineteenth-century community for the literary elite of Hartford. Two that are open to the public and worth seeing are the homes of Harriet Beecher Stowe and Samuel Clemens (Mark Twain). The Beecher Stowe house exemplifies a conventional upper-middle-class Victorian home, whereas the more pretentious Twain house is a monument to his eccentricities. In both cases, many of the writers' personal effects have been preserved.

Among them are Stowe's original paintings, Twain's bed, and the dining room chair where he told fantastic tales for his guests and family. Tour guides recount humorous details from the authors' everyday lives. The guided tour of both homes takes approximately an hour and fifteen minutes. Admission is charged. If you're ready for lunch after Nook Farm, drive one mile into Hartford's center. The best selection of restaurants is found along Main Street.

▲▲ **Wadsworth Atheneum**—The Atheneum, at 600 Main Street in Hartford, was established in 1842 and is an art museum of national stature. Its American, European, contemporary, Baroque, and Renaissance collections are worth viewing. The museum is open Tuesday through Sunday from 11:00 a.m. to 5:00 p.m. Admission is $3 for adults, $1.50 for senior citizens, free for children under 12. Museum admission is free on Thursdays and on Saturdays from 11:00 a.m. to 1:00 p.m.

▲ **Goodspeed's Opera House**—Somewhat of an area landmark, this attractive building on the banks of the Connecticut River in East Haddam will catch your eye on the way to Gillette's Castle. Tours of the building are available, and should you decide to stay in the area awhile, the opera house hosts evening performances of popular musicals April through December. Performance tickets range from $17 to $25. You can dine prior to a performance next door at the Gelston House or picnic on the river's edge.

▲▲ **Gillette's Castle**—They say a man's home is his castle, and in actor William Gillette's case, that statement can be taken literally. Best known for his portrayal of Sherlock Holmes, Gillette built his castle overlooking the Connecticut River in Hadlyme. The jagged stone exterior of the castle is striking, yet other than several intricately carved wooden doors the interior is fairly modest. Children will no doubt enjoy exploring the castle, and theater buffs will appreciate the Broadway memorabilia on display. Admission, $1 for adults and $.50 for children under 12, is reasonable and won't break the family pocketbook. The castle grounds are a Connecticut state park, so there are picnic tables available as well as a souvenir shop and refreshment stand. Skip the wooded trail unless you are in the mood to stretch your legs. The castle is open daily from Memorial Day through Columbus Day from 10:00 a.m. to 5:00 p.m. and on weekends only Columbus Day through mid-December from 10:00 a.m. to 4:00 p.m.

▲ **River Museum**—On the waterfront at the end of Main Street in Essex, the museum's exhibits pertain to river history. The museum is open April through December Tuesday through Sunday from 10:00 a.m. to 5:00 p.m. Admission is $1.50 for adults, $.50 for children, and $1 for senior citizens.

▲▲ Steam Train and Riverboat Ride—On Railroad Avenue in Essex, this excursion offers a good alternative for seeing the Connecticut River and sights such as Gillette's Castle and Goodspeed's Opera House if you're tired of driving or if you fancy steam-powered locomotives. All trains connect with a riverboat cruise, except for the last train of the day. Tickets cost $6.95 for adults and $2.95 for children for the one-hour train ride only, or $9.95 for adults and $4.95 per child for the train and riverboat trip combined. The combined trip takes over two hours, and children under two years of age ride free. You cannot buy separate tickets for the riverboat cruise. The service operates from late April through Christmas. Call ahead for departure times, as they vary from day to day and from season to season (203-767-0103).

Lodging

The Tourist Information Center at the Mystic exit will help you find lodging. The center has a board listing nearby accommodations, their rates and driving distances. The center's helpful personnel will even call ahead to secure your room. While you're at the center, be sure to peruse the menus from area restaurants and pick out the ones that best suit your tastes and budget. The tourist center is also a great source of area sightseeing information.

The **Inn at Mystic**, at the junction of Route 27 and US 1, has accommodations ranging from motor court rooms to comfortable rooms in a traditional country inn. There are gardens, a tennis court, a restaurant, a pool, and a hot tub on the premises. Call (800) 237-2415 or (203) 536-9604.

If you wish to stay within walking distance of Mystic's downtown shops and restaurants, the **Whaler's Inn**, offering simple, motel-like accommodations and senior citizen discounts, is the only lodging establishment in Mystic's center. Call (203) 536-1506.

Camping

Seaport Campgrounds, three miles from Mystic Seaport Museum, is the closest campground to Mystic's attractions. From the Mystic exit, #90 on Interstate 95, take Route 27 north for one and a quarter miles to Route 184. Follow Route 184 East for about one-half mile and watch for the campground on your left. RV hookups and tent sites are available, as well as complete recreational facilities on the premises, including swimming and fishing. Call (203) 536-4461 for reservations. Open seasonally mid-April through late October.

Dining

The Griswold Inn, Essex, serves sandwiches and burgers for
lunch and traditional New England fare for dinner in a lively
atmosphere. A fine collection of firearms and maritime prints
dot the walls of the Griswold's several dining rooms. Lunch is
about $8 per person and dinner entrées run from $15 to $20.
Servings are hearty. The inn also has 23 guest rooms. Reservations are recommended for overnight lodging or weekend dinners. Call (203) 767-1812.

In the Mystic area, you'll find a number of reasonably priced
restaurants and fast-food establishments in and around Olde
Mystick Village, just off I-95. A variety of restaurants can be
found in downtown Mystic itself. **Mulligan's**, on the west side
of the drawbridge in Mystic, has moderately priced meals ranging from sandwiches to lobster. On the opposite side of the
drawbridge, **The Landing**'s menu is predominantly seafood
(203-572-0549). Entrées start around $12. Locals recommend
The Draw Bridge Inne, ½ block from the drawbridge on
Main Street, offering specialties for both seafarers and landlubbers. Dinner entrées are $13 and up. For a simple but filling
meal, try an overstuffed sandwich at **2 Sisters Deli** on Pearl
Street just off Main. For breakfast, try **Bee Bee Dairy**, a family
style restaurant on Main Street, or **The Binnacle**, which has a
very casual atmosphere and filling breakfasts.

Itinerary Option

Those who wish to extend their New England vacation south-
ward to explore the exclusive Hamptons or the sand dunes at
Montauk can opt to take the ferry from New London, Connecticut (several miles south of Mystic), to Orient Point on Long
Island, New York. From Orient Point, take Route 25 West to
Riverhead, where you pick up Route 24. Follow Route 24 until it
intersects with Route 27. Drive east on Route 27 to the Hamptons, then continue all the way out to the lighthouse at Montauk
Point. The ferry costs $7.50 for adults, $4 for children, $22 for
most automobiles, including driver, and motor homes are $1.75
per foot. You really do need to bring your car across to do any
sightseeing. The rates quoted are for one-way passage, and the
ferry operates year-round. Call (203) 443-5281 for schedule and
reservation information. Sailing time is approximately one and a
half hours.

From New London, one can also take a ferry to lovely Block
Island. Reservations are required for automobiles. Call (203)
442-9553 for ferry information. Also, New York City is only two
hours south from New London on Interstate 95.

MYSTIC

Early New Englanders were dependent on the ocean for food, fuel, and goods brought from abroad. The importance of the sea comes to life in Mystic Seaport's re-creation of a nineteenth-century maritime village.

Suggested Schedule	
8:30 a.m.	Breakfast.
9:30 a.m.	Mystic Seaport Museum.
4:00 p.m.	Leave for Newport, Rhode Island.

Travel Route: Mystic to Newport (45 miles)
From Mystic's center, travel along coastal US 1 to Route 138 East. Cross over to Jamestown, then take the Jamestown toll bridge to Newport. Several miles north of Mystic you may want to take a short detour on Route 1A to see the well-preserved village of Stonington.

Sightseeing Highlights
▲▲▲ **Mystic Seaport Museum**—The entrance to the village is on Route 27 East less than one mile from I-95. You'll need the better part of a day to explore the museum grounds fully. In the village you can climb aboard a whaling vessel to see the cramped quarters of deck hands and where whale blubber was processed, visit seaport shops typical of those that would have served a fishing community one hundred years ago, watch boat-builders at work, learn how fishermen navigated by the stars in the planetarium, and see how sailing, once a necessary skill, has become a modern sport in a special tribute to the America's Cup. General admission to the village, at $11 for adults and $6 for children ages 5 to 18, is rather expensive, but considering the vast number of exhibits the Seaport has to offer, the money is well spent. Admission to the planetarium is $.75 additional for adults and $.50 for children. Steamboat cruises that leave from the village cost $2.50 for adults and $1.75 for kids. For a fast-food lunch of clam cakes, burgers, or hot dogs, there is a snack bar in the village; for more refined dining, try the **Seaman's Inne** next to the complex. The museum is open daily in the spring and summer from 9:00 a.m. to 5:00 p.m., during the fall and winter from 9:00 a.m. to 4:00 p.m.; closed Christmas Day.
▲ **Mystic Marinelife Aquarium**—Just off Route 95 at the Mystic Exit, this one is worthwhile if you didn't make it to the

New England Aquarium in Boston and have extra time after
visiting the Seaport. Entrance fees are $6.75 for adults, $3.75 for
children, and $5.75 for seniors. The aquarium opens daily at
9:00 a.m. Closed Thanksgiving, Christmas, and New Year's Day.
▲ **Denison Pequotsepos Nature Center**—The center, on
Pequotsepos Road in Mystic, is comprised of self-guided nature
trails and a small natural history museum. One trail is designed
especially for blind visitors. The center is open April through
October Monday through Saturday from 8:00 a.m. to 4:00 p.m.
and on Sundays from 1:00 p.m. to 5:00 p.m. During the winter
months it is open Tuesday through Saturday from 10:00 a.m. to
4:00 p.m. and Sundays from 1:00 p.m. to 4:00 p.m. A small
admission fee is charged.
Olde Mystic Village—It is probably best to pass on this group
of souvenir shops and informal eating establishments adjacent
to the aquarium unless you have plenty of time to kill.

Lodging
Stay in the heart of things at the **Inntowne** on the corner of
Thames and Mary streets. Although the inn was built within the
last ten years, it captures the feel of an old-fashioned inn, and
the shops and restaurants of Newport are at your doorstep. In-
season rates begin at $80 for a double. Call (401) 846-9200 for
reservations.

The newly built **Marriott** on the waterfront is also convenient to Newport's center. To make reservations, call Marriott's toll-free number (800) 228-9290 or the hotel directly at
(401) 849-1000. Nine of the Marriott's rooms are specially
equipped for handicapped guests. Doubles run about $195
nightly during the week and $165 on weekends if you ask for
their super saver weekend rate.

Nearby, on quiet Clarke Street but still in the center of Newport, is a row of three bed and breakfast establishments. The
Queen Anne at #16, built in the Victorian era, has an especially
friendly staff and offers reasonable accommodations with
shared bath starting at $45 per night, (401) 846-5676. The
Admiral Farragut (401-849-0640) at 31 Clarke was built in
1650, and the **Melville House** (401-847-0640) at 39 Clarke was
built in 1750. Both inns serve breakfast.

For a splurge you won't soon forget, stay at the **Inn at Castle
Hill** off Ocean Drive. With a room overlooking the ocean,
you'll almost feel like a Vanderbilt. Doubles with private bath
run $175 and suites $225 during the summer. Rooms are about
$100 less per night during the winter months. The inn's restau-
rant is also well worth a try (401-849-3800).

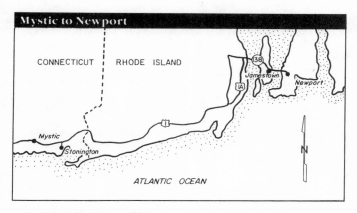

Mystic to Newport

CONNECTICUT   RHODE ISLAND
Jamestown
Newport
Mystic
Stonington
ATLANTIC OCEAN

Bed & Breakfast of Rhode Island, (401) 849-1298, can also help you locate accommodations. Their service is free of charge.

Camping
There are several municipal campgrounds near Newport, the closest being **Middletown Campground** on Second Beach in neighboring Middletown. Since there are only 44 campsites, reservations are strongly recommended. Call (401) 846-5781. Open May through early October. It has toilets, showers, and sewer hookups.

On the far side of the island, **Melville Ponds Campground** off Route 114 in Portsmouth has tent sites, RV sites with hook-ups, and recreational facilities. Open April 1 through October 31. Call (401) 849-8212.

If all campgrounds on the island are filled, try the camp-ground in Jamestown at **Fort Getty Recreation Area**. You can fish at the campground, but you will have to cross the toll bridge to sightsee in Newport. It is open only during the sum-mer months; call (401) 423-1363 for reservation information.

Dining
The **Black Pearl** (401-846-5264) on Bannister's Wharf is a very popular Newport restaurant, as evidenced by the throngs of hungry diners in line to be seated. Because of its reputation, the restaurant can be crowded and the service slow. Next door at the **Clarke Cooke House** (401) 849-2900 you'll find truly ele-gant dining upstairs for dinner and more casual atmosphere downstairs at the **Candy Store**. For dining in unique settings,

try the **S.S. Newport** on Waites Wharf, a floating restaurant that prides itself on its fresh seafood dishes (401-846-1200); the **La Forge Restaurant**, overlooking the grass courts at the Newport Casino, serving veal and chicken dinner entrées that run about $10; **The Moorings**, situated in the famous New York Yacht Club on Sayer's Wharf (401-846-2260); or the **White Horse Tavern**, the oldest operating tavern in the United States (410-849-3600). Numerous restaurants along Thames Street offer cheaper alternatives for eating out.

For dessert, visit any one of the **Newport Creamery**'s several locations for a traditional ice cream cone. **Poor Richard's** at 254 Thames Street is the place to get breakfast, from pancakes to omelets.

NEWPORT

Newport, on Aquidneck Island, is a city of contrasts—from the wealthy, some of whom still inhabit turn-of-the-century mansions, to military personnel stationed at the naval base, to the yachting crowd that routinely invades Newport each summer. Somehow this city manages to satisfy all of these groups in their varied pursuits. Today you'll discover why.

Suggested Schedule

9:00 a.m.	Breakfast.
10:00 a.m.	Tour one of Newport's sumptuous mansions.
11:30 a.m.	Take Ocean Drive and stop for a picnic lunch at Brenton Point State Park.
1:00 p.m.	Visit another luxurious "cottage."
2:30 p.m.	Promenade along the Cliff Walk, skirting the great lawns of many of Newport's finest homes and the ocean some thirty feet below.
3:30 p.m.	See the Tennis Hall of Fame or Touro Synagogue, or spend the rest of the afternoon browsing at the Brick Marketplace, Bannister's Wharf, or along Thames Street.
6:00 p.m.	Dinner.
8:00 p.m.	Relax to the beat of a local band in one of Newport's many bars or watch a jai alai match.

Travel Route
All of today's driving will be within Newport itself. Ocean Drive can be reached either from the downtown waterfront area by following the signs to Ocean Drive or by traveling past the mansions on Bellevue Avenue and taking a left when you get to the end of Bellevue.

Newport "Cottages"
The Preservation Society of Newport operates six exquisite mansions, or "cottages" as they were called by their original owners. You will probably have time to visit only two in one day. Take your pick:

Marble House, **Chateau-Sur-Mer**, and **The Elms** are open throughout the winter from 10:00 a.m. to 4:00 p.m. on weekends and are beautifully decorated for Christmas. Most of the other mansions are open weekends starting in April, and all are open daily throughout the summer, some till 7:00 p.m. Check with the Preservation Society (401-847-1000) for current hours.

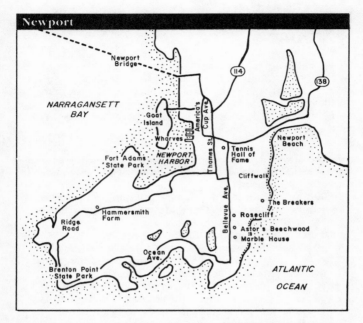

Admission to most of the mansions is $4.50 for adults and $2 for children ages 6 to 11. Reduced rates are available when you purchase combination tickets to more than one mansion.

The Breakers, on Ochre Point Avenue off Bellevue, is the most extravagant of all the mansions and the most popular with tourists. Built in an Italian Renaissance style for Cornelius Vanderbilt in 1895, the opulence of this stately home with an abundance of gold leaf and marble throughout its interior is almost overwhelming. Children will enjoy the children's cottage on the grounds.

Chateau-Sur-Mer (House-by-the-Sea) and **Rosecliff** are situated on the ocean as well. Chateau-Sur-Mer has a Chinese Moon Gate on its grounds. Rosecliff was designed by well-known architect Stanford White and has the largest private ballroom in Newport. Robert Redford and Mia Farrow waltzed in this ballroom in the movie version of *The Great Gatsby*.

Marble House on Bellevue Avenue is my personal favorite. Named appropriately for the beautiful and rare marble throughout, the "cottage" was built for William K. Vanderbilt in 1892. A Chinese teahouse on the grounds exemplifies the moneyed class's fascination with the Orient at the turn of the century.

Also on Bellevue Avenue are **The Elms** and **Kingscote**. The Elms, modeled after a French chateau, is known for its array of trees and shrubbery. Kingscote, built in 1839, is one of the oldest mansions open to the public. Incorporating elements of both Victorian and Gothic style architecture, the estate was named after William Henry King, who acquired the property in 1864.

Several other stately homes, not operated by the Preservation Society, are also open to the public. **Hammersmith Farms**, near Fort Adams, is considered the most "livable" of the Newport mansions. The wedding reception for John F. and Jackie Kennedy was held here. Its colorful gardens were designed by Frederick Law Olmsted. Open weekends in March and November and daily April through October from 10:00 a.m. to 5:00 p.m. At the height of the summer season hours are extended to 7:00 p.m.

Bellecourt Castle on Bellevue Avenue is still owned and occupied by the Tinney family. The house is open for tours by guides in period costume and for high teas. A gold coronation coach and art treasures from all over the world are among the items on display. Admission is $4.50 for adults, $3.50 for seniors, $3 for students, $1.50 for children ages 6 to 12. A family plan admits two adults and their children for $10. The house is closed January through mid-February and is open daily from 9:00 a.m. to 5:00 p.m. during the summer. Call (401) 846-0669 for museum hours if you plan to visit during the spring or fall.

Beechwood, also on Bellevue, was built for the Astors. Although the home is not as lavish or well kept as the Preservation Society mansions, the tour can be quite entertaining: actors playing members of the Astor household greet you as a dinner guest and treat you to family gossip of the day. A "calling card" is $5 for adults. The house is open daily June through October. For hours, call (401) 846-3772.

The grand mansions of Newport are not the only homes that merit a look while you're here. There are many beautifully restored colonial homes in and around Queen Anne Square one block from Thames Street. Explore these streets on your own or take an organized walking tour with the Newport Historical Society. The society is located at 82 Touro Street, and tours are $3 for everyone over the age of 12. The tours begin at 10:00 a.m. in the summer. Call (401) 846-0813 for additional information.

Other Sightseeing Highlights
▲ **Touro Synagogue**—Built in 1763, the oldest synagogue in the country is now a National Historic Site. Summer hours are 10:00 a.m. to 5:00 p.m. daily, except Saturdays. Winter visitors should call (401) 847-4794 for an appointment.
▲ **Tennis Hall of Fame**—The museum is adjacent to the emerald-green grass courts of the Newport Casino. The casino

was built in 1880, and professional tennis tournaments are still held there today. Admission to the museum is $4 for adults, $2 for youths under 16, or $10 per family. Senior citizen discounts are available. The museum is open from 10:00 a.m. to 5:00 p.m. May through October and 11:00 a.m. to 4:00 p.m. the rest of the year.

▲ **Green Animals**—These topiary gardens are on Cory's Lane off Route 114 North in Portsmouth. An elephant, giraffe, and camel are just a few of the animal-shaped shrubs that are bound to amuse children and adults alike. Operated by the Preservation Society of Newport, the estate is open daily May through September from 10:00 a.m. to 5:00 p.m. and throughout October on weekends only. Admission is $4 for adults, $2 for children ages 6 to 11.

Should you wish to view the island from a two-wheeled vehicle, you can rent bicycles from **Ten Speed Spokes** at the corner of Elm and America's Cup Avenue (401-847-5609) or mopeds from **Newport Rent-a-Ped, Ltd.**, on Waites Wharf (401-846-7788).

Shopping

The Brick Marketplace on Thames Street and Bannister's and Bowen wharves off America's Cup Avenue comprise Newport's main shopping district. Not to be missed by nautical buffs is the **Armchair Sailor Bookstore** on Lee's Wharf, which has one of the most comprehensive selections anywhere of maritime publications.

Nightlife

Jai alai is considered to be the fastest game on two feet. Rhode Island is one of the few states that allows pari-mutuel wagering on the sport, and you may wish to view a match or two of this exciting game at **Newport Jai Alai**, 150 Admiral Kalbfus Road. Admission is nominal to encourage betting, which some find similar to playing the horses. Dial (800) 556-6900 nationwide or (800) 451-2500 within Rhode Island for information.

Many of Newport's bars and restaurants offer musical entertainment in the evenings. Try **The Ark** on Thames Street for jazz. **Cobblestones**, also on Thames, has live entertainment on weekends and a piano bar. **Gatsby's** on America's Cup Avenue is the place to go for dancing to a contemporary beat.

NEW BEDFORD AND SANDWICH

Leaving Newport's tycoons behind, today you'll learn about more customary nineteenth-century New England occupations, such as whaling in New Bedford and glass-making in Sandwich.

9:00 a.m.	Leave Newport for New Bedford.
10:00 a.m.	Visit Whaling Museum.
11:00 a.m.	Stroll through New Bedford's renovated historic district and sit down to an early lunch.
12:30 p.m.	Travel to Cape Cod.
1:30 p.m.	Sandwich Glass Museum.
2:30 p.m.	Heritage Plantation.
5:00 p.m.	Check into lodging.
6:00 p.m.	Early dinner and quiet evening to prepare for an early departure in the morning.

Travel Route: Newport to Sandwich (62 miles)
From Newport, take Route 114 North to Route 24 North toward Tiverton and Fall River. At Fall River get on Interstate 195 East toward Cape Cod. Get off at Exit 15 onto Route 18 for New Bedford's historic quarter and follow signs to the Visitor Center.

After stopping in New Bedford, return to I-195 East. Take exit 22A for Route 25 for Cape Cod and the islands. Stay on Route 25 across the Bourne Bridge. There is a rotary at the end of the bridge. Follow the rotary three-quarters of the way around to US 6 East toward Sagamore. As you approach the Sagamore Bridge, go straight onto Route 6A East for Sagamore and Sandwich. When you get to Sandwich, there will be a sign to the center, which is about one-half mile from Route 6A to your right.

New Bedford Sightseeing Highlights
Once a bustling whaling center, New Bedford experienced a great decline during the twentieth century. Recently, efforts have been made to restore the city to its past glory. You can see the handsome result of those efforts by rambling through the sixteen-block cobblestone area that comprises the historic district, originally built in the 1760s. In its heyday, 10,000 men from New Bedford made their living in the whaling trade. New

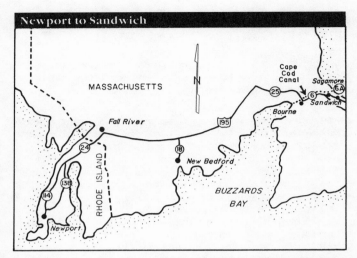

Newport to Sandwich

Bedford's visitor center is on Second Street in the historic district. Hours of operation are Monday through Saturday 9:00 a.m. to 5:00 p.m. and Sundays 11:00 a.m. to 5:00 p.m.

▲▲ **Whaling Museum**—Exhibits here, ranging from model vessels and ship's logs to artwork depicting whaling expeditions, will give you a fascinating look at an industry and an era that have long since died out. Open Monday through Saturday 9:00 a.m. to 5:00 p.m, Sundays 1:00 p.m. to 5:00 p.m. Admission is $3 for adults, $2 for children ages 6 to 14, and $2.50 for seniors. After visiting the museum, you may want to visit the **Seaman's Bethel** across the street: it was the whalemen's chapel referred to in Herman Melville's *Moby Dick*.

▲ **New Bedford Glass Museum**—The museum is located at 50 North Second Street opposite the Visitor Center. Over 1,000 pieces of glass and silver manufactured in the New Bedford area are displayed in a handsome nineteenth-century home. Sandwich's Glass Museum, which one might visit later in the day, has a more extensive glass collection. Open Monday through Saturday 10:00 a.m. to 5:00 p.m. and Sundays 1:00 p.m. to 4:00 p.m.; January through March the museum is closed Tuesday through Friday. Admission is $2 for adults, $1.50 for seniors, $.50 for children ages 6 to 12.

Sandwich Sightseeing Highlights
The town of Sandwich celebrated its 350th birthday in 1987. It is the quintessential Cape Cod town, with well-kept shingled houses, gentle tidal marshes, and many sights to occupy the out-of-town visitor.

▲▲ **Heritage Plantation**—The plantation is on Grove and Pine streets. To get there, take a left onto Grove Street next to the Town Hall in Sandwich Center. The parking lot will be on your left approximately one-half mile from Sandwich Center. The prettiest time to visit the plantation is in early June when the rhododendrons are in full bloom, but the beautifully landscaped, 76-acre grounds are handsome in any season. American folk art, Currier & Ives lithographs, antique firearms, and early automobiles are among the plantation's other attractions. The antique cars, housed in a replica of the Shaker round barn at Hancock, include a vibrant green and yellow Duesenberg designed for Gary Cooper which will delight auto buffs. The art museum houses a carousel to entertain the children while you view the Currier & Ives collection. Buses run at regular intervals between the museums. Admission is $6 for adults, $5 for seniors, $2.50 for children ages 5 to 12. The plantation is open from mid-May through late October from 10:00 a.m. to 5:00 p.m. daily, although tickets are not sold after 4:15 p.m. Picnicking on the grounds is not allowed.

▲ **Sandwich Glass Museum**—Across from the Town Hall Square in Sandwich Center, the museum houses a fine collection of glassware made in the 1800s by the Boston & Sandwich Glass Company and the Cape Cod Glass Works. Exhibits include an explanation of glass manufacturing procedures and a chronology of the Sandwich operation. Open daily from 9:30 a.m. to 4:30 p.m. April through October. The museum is closed during January and open the remaining months Wednesday through Sunday from 9:30 a.m. to 4:00 p.m. Admission is $2.50 for adults, $.50 for children over five.

In Sandwich, one can also visit a water-operated stone **Grist Mill**, admission $1.25 for adults, $.75 for children ages 12 to 16; **Yesteryears Doll Museum** in the First Parish Meetinghouse; and several historic homes, including the **Thornton Burgess Museum**, which was the home of the author of children's books, admission by donation. All are within a three-block radius of Town Hall Square. Book lovers will enjoy the **Wisdom and Whimsey Bookshop** on Main Street about a block and a half south of the Dan'l Webster Inn.

Lodging
On Sandwich's Main Street, the **Dan'l Webster Inn** (508-888-3622) will bathe you in four-star comfort you won't have to sell your soul for. The distinguished dining room is reputed to serve the best baked stuffed lobster on the Cape. Reservations are recommended. **Six Water Street** (508-888-6808) next to the Thornton Burgess Museum, **Captain Ezra Nye Guesthouse** (508-888-6142) across the street from the Dan'l Webster, **The**

Quince Tree Inn (508-888-1371), and **Isaiah Jones Homestead** (508-888-9115) are all bed-and-breakfast type establishments right in Sandwich Center.

You'll find a wide assortment of motor inns and cottages along scenic 6A in Sandwich. On the upper end is the mock Tudor-style **Earl of Sandwich Motor Manor** (508-888-1415). The **Spring Garden Motor Inn** (508-888-0710) in East Sandwich is on the edge of a tidal marsh, and the more expensive **Wingscorton Farm Inn** (508-888-0534) offers accommodations on an antique working farm.

For those traveling on a budget, the **HyLand Youth Hostel** is in nearby Hyannis not far from the ferry boat docks. The hostel is open all year and also offers facilities for families and couples. Call (508) 775-2970 for information.

Camping
Shawme Crowell State Forest on Route 130 in Sandwich has 270 sites and is open seasonally (508-888-0351).

Dining
For lunch in New Bedford, there is a bakery adjacent to the visitor's center which serves croissant sandwiches. **Freestone's Restaurant Bar & Grill**, in an attractive building on the corner of Williams and Second streets, serves seafood melt sandwiches and the like at reasonable prices; entrées are more expensive at around $12 apiece. **Jimmy Connor's Irish Pub** is a good place to stop for a casual burger and draft beer at a modest price on the corner of Acushnet and Union streets. The **Last Laugh** is a bar and deli just north of the historic district where you can sample sandwiches named for famous comedians such as Jackie Gleason.

For dinner, if the Dan'l Webster is too steep for your budget, try **Sandy's** (508-888-6480), a family-style restaurant just north of Sandwich on Route 6A. The fried clams are marvelous, but bring a hearty appetite as the portions are huge. Just a little farther north on Route 6A is the **Sagamore Inn** (508-888-9707), a favorite with locals. The atmosphere is very lively, and the fare ranges from fresh seafood to New England style dinners and Italian specialties.

Itinerary Options
Bargain hunters with time to spare may profit from prospecting the New Bedford/Fall River area factory outlet stores. These stores are factory outlets in the truest sense, since they are generally located on the premises of the factory. A guide to the outlets can be picked up at the New Bedford Visitor Center.

MARTHA'S VINEYARD

Although much of your New England trip so far has been spent along the coastline, where day-to-day life in the past was tied to the ocean and in some areas still is, you'll spend the next two days visiting islands whose main lifeline to "civilization" is the sea. The itinerary is planned so that you can spend one day each on the islands of Martha's Vineyard and Nantucket. However, the islands are meant to be toured at a relaxed pace, so you may want to travel to just one island and spread its sightseeing highlights out over two days—or allow more time on each island. The interisland ferry only runs from early July through mid-September, so if you are traveling during any other month, you will probably have to limit yourself to just one island.

Suggested Schedule

8:15 a.m.	Leave Sandwich for Hyannis docks.
9:15 a.m.	Ferry leaves for Martha's Vineyard.
11:00 a.m.	Arrive in Vineyard Haven and travel to Gay Head.
12:30 p.m.	Have lunch and see the jagged cliffs at Gay Head.
1:30 p.m.	Leave Gay Head for Edgartown.
2:30 p.m.	Take your choice: stroll past stately mansions from the whaling era or shop for souvenirs in lovely Edgartown; or soak up the sun on a quiet beach on Chappaquiddick or along Beach Road between Edgartown and Oak Bluffs.
6:00 p.m.	Check into accommodations.
7:00 p.m.	Dinner.

Travel Route: Sandwich to Ferry Docks in Hyannis (10 miles)

From Sandwich Center, travel to Hyannis by taking Route 6A East until it intersects with Route 132. Turn right onto Route 132. When you reach Hyannis, there will be a rotary and signs to the ferry docks. (If you plan to travel to Nantucket or Martha's Vineyard for the day only, there is free parking on South Street about two blocks from the docks. The parking lots are marked by a blue shell sign with a large P in the center of the shell. Cars may not be left overnight in the free parking lots.) Long-term parking at the docks costs about $6 per day. Should you wish to bring your car to Martha's Vineyard, you'll need to take the ferry from Woods Hole, which is described below as a route option.

Steamship Authority boats leave from South Street and travel to and from Nantucket only; Hy-Line Boats to both Nantucket and Martha's Vineyard leave from Ocean Street, which intersects with South Street. Because of their proximity to one another and because fares from Nantucket ($9.50 for adults, and $4.75 for children) are roughly the same on both lines, it is possible to take the Hy-Line out to the islands and return by the Steamship Authority, or vice versa, giving you more departure times to choose from. Sailing time from Hyannis is approximately one hour and 45 minutes to Vineyard Haven and roughly two hours to Nantucket (some of the Hy-Line boats can do it in an hour and 45 minutes).

You will arrive on Martha's Vineyard in Vineyard Haven. Rent a moped and ride southwest toward West Tisbury. From West Tisbury, travel along Middle Road to Chilmark, and from Chilmark follow signs to Gay Head. If you're picnicking, turn right about five miles outside of Chilmark at the sign for Lobsterville Beach. After lunch, return to the main road and continue to Gay Head to view the cliffs and lighthouse. If you didn't bring a picnic lunch, there are several fast-food establishments at Gay Head where you can get fried clam platters and the like. It is 19 miles from Vineyard Haven to Gay Head.

From Gay Head, return to West Tisbury, then follow the Edgartown-West Tisbury Road to Edgartown. The total distance from Gay Head to Edgartown is 21 miles.

Route Option: Visiting Martha's Vineyard one day and Nantucket the next, which involves a lot of travel time on ferries and the added expense of renting alternative modes of transportation on the islands, may not allow as much time as one might like to explore each island. Should you decide to visit only Martha's Vineyard, take the ferry from Woods Hole instead of from Hyannis. It is faster and cheaper. To get to Woods Hole from Sandwich, take Route 6A West to Sagamore. At Sagamore follow US 6 West to Bourne. From Bourne, take Route 28 East to Falmouth and follow signs to the docks. The first ferry to the Vineyard usually leaves around 7:00 a.m. in the summer, and sailing time is approximately 45 minutes. Boats leaving from Woods Hole arrive in either Oak Bluffs or Vineyard Haven, only a few miles apart.

Passenger fares from Woods Hole to Martha's Vineyard are about $4 for adults and $2 for children one way. Automobiles are $26.50 one way from mid-May through mid-October and about half that during the winter months. Reservations for automobiles are *strongly* recommended during the summer months. Although it may seem expensive to bring a car over, when you consider that mopeds rentals are $50 a day during the summer season, it may be worth the fare, particularly if you decide to stay more than one day or if there are more than two people in your party. Call the Steamship Authority in Woods Hole (508-540-2022) for ferry schedule and reservation information.

Should you wish to spend all your time on Nantucket instead, call either Hy-Line Cruises (508-778-2600) or the Steamship Authority (508-771-4000) in Hyannis for complete ferry information. Cars can travel on Steamship Authority ferries only, at a rate of $66.50 one way. Since Nantucket is such a small island, it really makes most sense to leave your car on the mainland and travel by other means once on the island.

Transportation on Martha's Vineyard

Mopeds are one of the easiest ways to get around the island— you don't have to worry about finding a parking space when you discover that deserted stretch of beach, and you can travel much faster than on a bicycle. The suggested schedule is designed for those traveling by moped; if you decide to bicycle instead, adjust your travel time accordingly. There are clearly marked and well-maintained bicycle paths on the island.

Moped and bicycle rental places abound in Vineyard Haven, Edgartown, and particularly Oak Bluffs. Many operations claim they have the lowest rates on the island. You may want to shop around, but my experience has been that rates tend to be fairly consistent from one place to the next and that your time is better spent sightseeing than looking for a bargain-priced moped rental. Daily rentals cost about $50 in season and $40 in the off-season for a moped that seats two fairly comfortably. Bicycle rentals run about $10 to $15 per day.

Lagoon Rentals (508-693-7766), on Beach Road opposite the New Bedford and Boston ferry dock in Vineyard Haven, is run by the same people who run **Simon Rentals** (508-693-7543) in Oak Bluffs, so you can pick up your bike or moped when you arrive in Vineyard Haven and return it in Oak Bluffs just before getting on the ferry to Nantucket. This will save you the cost of a taxi ride after you return your vehicle.

Numerous taxi services and sightseeing operators will greet you right at the boat and take you around the island, should you not want to get around on your own steam.

Martha's Vineyard

Though Martha's Vineyard is only seven miles from Cape Cod and the mainland, once you get there it doesn't take long to relax and leave the rest of the world behind. The island is 20

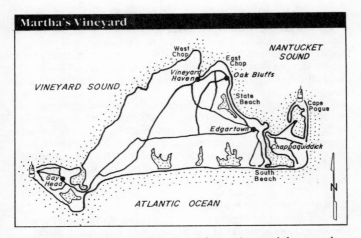

miles long by 10 miles wide at its widest point, and the popula-
tion swells from around 12,000 year-round residents to almost
62,000 during the summer. Even so, if you venture out of the
main towns, you can almost always find a quiet spot to call
your own.

Martha's Vineyard was named for an early settler's daughter
and for the abundance of grapes that used to cover the island.
Now the island is comprised of three main towns—Vineyard
Haven, Oak Bluffs, and Edgartown—with stretches of white
sand beach and sand dunes in between. Edgartown, the most
elegant of the three, is another example of what great prosperity
the whaling trade brought to nineteenth-century New England
communities. Vineyard Haven is the quietest of the three, while
Oak Bluffs, with its colorful Victorian "gingerbread" houses and
active nightlife, is the most flamboyant.

Most people don't come to Martha's Vineyard to spend their
time in museums, but if inclement weather forces you indoors,
there is the **Old Schoolhouse Museum** on Main Street in
Vineyard Haven run by the Historical Preservation Society. The
museum is open Monday through Friday from 10:00 a.m. to
2:00 p.m.; admission is by donation. Also in Vineyard Haven,
The Jirah Luce House displays nautical and other artifacts
representing nineteenth-century island life, including a collection of Victorian dolls. The museum is on Beach Street and is
open Tuesday through Saturday from 10:00 a.m. to 4:30 p.m.
Admission is $2 for adults and $.50 for children. In Edgartown
on School Street, the **Dukes County Historical Society**
operates a museum and library dedicated to preserving island
history through its exhibits of maritime artifacts, scrimshaw,

and antique clothing. Indoor island activities include shopping in Edgartown or, if you're traveling with kids, visiting the **Flying Horses Carousel** at the bottom of Circuit Avenue in Oak Bluffs.

Back outdoors, some may enjoy an excursion to **Chappaquiddick Island**. A ferry runs from the waterfront in Edgartown to the island from 7:30 a.m. to midnight during the summer. One-way fares are $1.75 for car and driver, $.35 for each passenger, $1 for bicycle and rider, $1.50 for mopeds and motorcycles, and in case you brought yours along, horses and cattle are $.75 each. The ferry, which runs as needed, must be one of the shortest ferry crossings you'll ever experience. Moped riders may not find the trip worthwhile, since the main road turns to sand several miles inland, and mopeds are not meant to operate in sand. The Chappaquiddick Bridge is on the far side of the island.

The beaches on the Vineyard are lovely, and perhaps the most accessible beach to the public is the **Joseph Silvia State Beach**, which runs along the road between Edgartown and Oak Bluffs. Just park your vehicle on the side of the road, hop over the dunes, and stretch out. Warning: as tempting as it may be, overnight camping is not allowed.

Helpful Hints
Those who plan to travel about the island by bicycle or moped should only bring over one small bag that will fit easily on one's back or in the vehicle's basket. If you need to carry more than a daypack, be prepared to take a taxi to and from your hotel once on the island.

Lodging
For sumptuous accommodations, the **Charlotte Inn** on South Summer Street fits the bill, providing country inn comfort in restored nineteenth-century homes that originally belonged to sea captains. Doubles start at $115 and suites at $195 during the high season and begin at $55 for a double or $105 for a suite from mid-October through early May (508-627-4751). The lovely **Victorian Inn** on South Water Street was once a whaling captain's home as well and is now listed in the National Register of Historic Places. Prices are more moderate than at the Charlotte, and breakfast is included (508-627-4784). Two other handsome bed and breakfasts are the **Daggett House** at 59 North Water Street (508-627-4600), with its secret stairway, and the **Governor Bradford Inn** at 128 Main Street (508-627-9510), also a captain's home. In season, doubles start at around $90 at both establishments.

The **Oak Bluffs Inn**, at the corner of Circuit Avenue and Pequot Avenue in Oak Bluffs, is painted flamboyantly in pink to exemplify the lighter side of Victorian architecture. Doubles begin at $90 during the summer (508-693-7171). The **Wesley Hotel** on Lake Avenue overlooking Oak Bluffs Harbor has recently been restored and is typical of many turn-of-the-century seaside hotels. Double rooms run between $90 and $120 during peak tourist season (508-693-6611).

The **Vineyard Harbor Motel**, on Beach Road leaving Vineyard Haven in the direction of Edgartown, sits on the harbor and has a nice courtyard; rooms are equipped with refrigerators (508-693-3334). The **Captain Dexter House** on Upper Main Street in Vineyard Haven was built in 1843 for a sea captain and now serves as a comfortable inn. Doubles run about $80 per night in season (508-693-6564).

Perhaps the least expensive lodging on the island can be found at the **Manter Memorial AYH Hostel** on the Edgartown-West Tisbury Road three miles west of the airport. Dormitory-style accommodations cost about $8 per night per person. The hostel is open from April through November, and you can call (508) 693-2665 for further information.

Camping

There are two campgrounds on Martha's Vineyard: **Webb Camping Area** on Barnes Road several miles southwest of Oak Bluffs (508-693-0233) and **Martha's Vineyard Family Campground** on the Edgartown-Vineyard Haven road a little over a mile from the ferry dock (508-693-3772). Martha's Vineyard Family Campground, the more conveniently located of the two, is open from mid-May through mid-October; it is also the more expensive, with nightly rates starting at $18. Webb Camping Area is open from mid-May through mid-September with nightly rates starting at $15. Both campgrounds have facilities for RV and tent campers.

Dining

During the summer, the visitor has plenty of dining choices on the island. There are a number of family-style restaurants and coffee shops along Vineyard Haven's Main Street, but since it is a "dry town," restaurants cannot serve liquor. **Classic Capers Cuisine,** on Beach Road in Vineyard Haven, can set you up with a picnic lunch, including gourmet pasta salads and sandwiches.

In Edgartown, the **Navigator Restaurant and Boathouse Bar** (508-627-4320) at the foot of Main Street and the **Wharf Restaurant** (508-627-9967) across the street both serve seafood. The Navigator overlooks the water, and lunches go for about $7.95, while dinner entrées run around $18.95. **Martha's**

Restaurant (508-627-8316), on Main Street across from the town hall, and **Over Martha's Cafe** upstairs are pleasant for either lunch or dinner. At lunch, Martha's Restaurant serves tasty sandwiches for about $7. Dinners lean toward pasta and seafood dishes in the $15 to $20 range. Over Martha's Cafe has a sushi and raw bar. Both are in an attractive Victorian dwelling with cheerful porch dining. If your appetite runs to entrées such as roast rack of lamb dijon, veal scaloppine, and prime rib, try the **Shiretown Inn & Restaurant** (508-627-3353). Dinner entrées start at $20, and there is a pub on the premises. **Andrea's Restaurant** (508-627-5850) on Upper Main Street features northern Italian cuisine in an elegant, but comfortable, setting, while **Jo Jo's** (508-627-3325) in the Colonial Inn complex on North Water Street serves more traditional Italian dishes such as manicotti and ravioli for take-out or sit-down meals at reasonable prices. For the cheapest oceanfront table in town, get a burger or fried clams to go from the **Quarterdeck** stand near the Chappaquiddick ferry and sit on the docks.

In Oak Bluffs, meals are usually casual and you can get anything from steak and seafood at **David's Island House** on Circuit Avenue; or you can get subs, pasta, and pizza at **Papa's Pizza** on upper Circuit Avenue, fresh fish at the **Oyster Bar** on Circuit, and Szechuan food at the **Orient Express** also on Circuit Avenue; or try the salads at the **Veg-Out Salad Bar** on Lake Avenue or Mexican food at **Zaboltec** (508-693-6800) on Kennbec Avenue.

Nightlife

Of the three main towns, Oak Bluffs has the most active nightlife on the Vineyard. The **Atlantic Connection Dance Club**, as well as some of the neighboring bars on Circuit Avenue, can be jam-packed during the summer months. Many of the patrons are college students working on the island during school break.

NANTUCKET

Thirty miles from the Massachusetts coast, Nantucket Island is a sparkling oasis in the Atlantic. Evidence of the island's one-time prominence in whaling can be seen in the facades of graceful Federal, Greek Revival, and Georgian style homes that border Nantucket town's cobblestone streets. Shingled cottages in Siasconset on the other side of the island are more modest, yet no less respectable, reminders of the seafaring life. In between are miles of low-lying moors and soft sand beaches.

Suggested Schedule

9:00 a.m.	Stroll around Oak Bluffs.
10:00 a.m.	Take ferry to Nantucket.
12:00 noon	Arrive in Nantucket and travel to Siasconset.
1:00 p.m.	Picnic on the beach in Siasconset.
3:00 p.m.	Return to the town of Nantucket and spend the rest of the afternoon exploring quaint narrow streets, attractive boutiques, and historic homes.
7:00 p.m.	Dinner.

Travel Route

Bay State Provincetown Cruises (617-723-7800) operates an interisland ferry from Oak Bluffs, Martha's Vineyard, to Nantucket during July, August, and September. The ferry takes passengers only. It departs from Oak Bluffs at 10:00 a.m. and costs $10 for adults and $5 for children.

Once on Nantucket, travel to Siasconset by following Main Street away from the docks to Orange Street. Turn left onto Orange Street and follow it until you come to a rotary. At the rotary, take Milestone Road all the way to Siasconset. Affectionately known as "Sconset," Siasconset is 7½ miles from the town of Nantucket. For bicyclists, a paved bike path parallels the main road for most of the distance.

Sightseeing Highlights

In Siasconset, there are no official sights to see, but the town's often-deserted beach, quiet seaside lanes, and charming weathered cottages are enough to warrant the trip from Nantucket Center. One of my favorite walks is along the footpath that runs between some of Sconset's most beautiful homes and

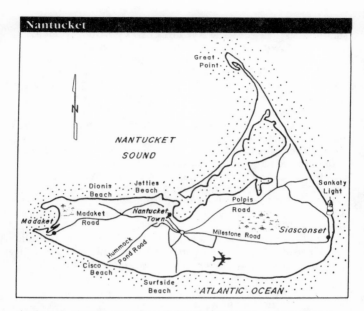

the beach plum covered sand dunes that serve as a protective
barrier between the houses and the sea. To get to the footpath,
go straight from the market in the town's center to the row of
houses overlooking the beach. At the end of the row is a house
named "Casa Marina"; turn right just to the left of "Casa
Marina" on what looks like a driveway. Where the driveway
veers back to the main road, continue straight ahead onto the
lawn. This is the beginning of the footpath. The path will lead
you across people's lawns—which is legal, but be considerate of
their property. The path runs from the village out to Sankaty
Head Lighthouse.

The **Nantucket Historical Association** operates five
period homes, as well as nine museums and monuments,
representing four centuries of Nantucket history. The sights are
located throughout the town of Nantucket, so you should pick
up the "Historic Nantucket" brochure, which maps out the
route, from the tourist office on the corner of Chestnut Street,
just one block from Main Street.

The tour begins at the **Whaling Museum** on Broad Street
near Steamboat Wharf, then continues next door to the **Peter
Fougler Museum**, where a broader range of island artifacts is
on display along with a collection of handwoven Nantucket
lightship baskets. The period homes include the **Oldest**

House, built in 1686 and considered to be the oldest house still standing on the island; the **Nathaniel Macy House**, built in 1723; the **Hawden House**, a stately Greek Revival built in 1844 at the height of the whaling era; the **1800 House**; and **Greater Light**, converted from a barn into a summer cottage during the 1930s. You can also visit the **Old Gaol**, or old jail, built in 1805; the **Abiah Folger Franklin Memorial** on the site where Ben Franklin's mother was born; the **Old Mill**, built in 1746 and still operational today; the **Thomas Macy Warehouse**, originally constructed to prepare whaling vessels for their journeys; the **Quaker Meeting House**, dating to 1838; the **Fair Street Museum** next door, containing Nantucket decorative arts exhibits; and the **Fire Hose Cart House**, which houses nineteenth-century firefighting equipment and was built in 1866.

Admission charges to the various buildings range from $1 to $2.50, or you can get a visitor's pass that will admit you to all of them for $6.50 for adults and $2.50 for children ages 5 to 14. You'll need at least three hours to take the entire tour. The buildings close at 5:00 p.m., so if you wish to visit them all, you will probably have to pass on the trip to Sconset or else travel to Sconset late in the day.

The **Maria Mitchell Science Center**, dedicated to the nation's first prominent woman astronomer, operates a science library, a small natural science museum, an aquarium, and an observatory and maintains the astronomer's birthplace. Stop in at the library at 2 Vestal Street or call (508) 228-0898 for details.

Those with extra time to beachcomb may also want to visit **Children's Beach**, **Jetties Beach**, and **South Beach**, all within walking distance from downtown Nantucket. **Dionis Beach**, three miles south of town has still-water swimming, while more adventurous swimmers will enjoy the surf at **Madaket**, **Surfside**, and **Siasconset**. Serious surfers find **Cisco Beach** to their liking.

Helpful Hints

Nantucket is a small and flat enough island so that you can get around rather easily by bicycle. Rentals cost about $10 per day, and you should have no trouble locating the rental shops as you come off the boat. Moped rentals are much more expensive— $50 per day for a two-person moped. However, renting one allows you to cover much more ground in a short period of time. Most bike rental establishments also offer mopeds.

Bus service runs from Nantucket Center to Siasconset and other island beaches during the summer, or you may find it more convenient to explore the island by taxi or on a guided tour. **Barrett's Tours** on 20 Federal Street operates both a taxi service and guided tours. Call (508) 228-0174 for information.

Island Tours on Straight Wharf also runs island tours regularly from May through October (508-228-0334).

Lodging

In Sconset, your lodging choices are limited to **Wade Cottages** (508-257-6308) and the **Summer House Inn** (508-257-9976), which also has a restaurant. Both overlook the ocean and offer pleasant accommodations. Wade Cottages opens in late May and operates through September. Room rates range from $65 to $105. Lodging at the Summer House includes private sitting rooms. Prices start at $225 from mid-June to mid-September and at $125 off-season; the inn closes down for the season at the end of September.

The town of Nantucket has a seemingly endless list of bed and breakfasts, yet remarkably they fill up quickly during the height of the summer. The **Jared Coffin House** at 29 Broad Street, probably the best-known inn on the island, is open all year. Guest rooms are spread out among six dwellings, the oldest dating to the 1700s. The inn also operates a respectable restaurant, with courtyard dining in the summertime, and a cozy bar. Dining prices are moderate, while doubles go for $100 to $150 July through September and slightly less during the rest of the year (508-228-2400). The **Nesbitt Inn**, just down the block at 21 Broad Street in a large Victorian, is run by a friendly couple and is reasonably priced at $60 per night for a double (508-228-0156).

Lodgers will not be disappointed with the quality and comfort of **18 Gardner Street**, where double rooms rent for $90 to $130 nightly in summer, $55 to $90 nightly in winter (508-228-1155). The **Union Street Inn** (508-228-9222) at 7 Union is also lovely with rates comparable to 18 Gardner. There is a string of guest houses on North Water Street also convenient to the town center, such as the **Brass Lantern Inn** (508-228-4064) and the **Periwinkle Guesthouse** (508-228-9267). Room rates run from $50 to $140 at the Brass Lantern and from $65 to $110 at the Periwinkle.

There are no campgrounds on Nantucket, but **Star of the Sea AYH Hostel** in Surfside does give budget travelers a lodging option. Dormitory-style beds rent for $8 per night. Three and one-half miles from the ferry, the hostel is on the National Register of Historic Places, and its oceanside location is appealing. Reservations are essential (508-228-0433). The hostel is open April 1 through the end of October.

Dining

The **Sconset Cafe** (508-257-4008), in Siasconset Center, serves both lunch and dinner in addition to selling its own cookbook.

With entrées such as Indonesian grilled shrimp and shrimp stuffed artichokes, the café offers an interesting twist to its seafood dishes that one doesn't come across in too many New England restaurants. Lunch entrées run around $7, dinner entrées begin at around $17. The café is only open during the summer, as is the market around the corner where you can pick up fresh sandwiches and pasta or potato salad to take down to the beach with you.

The **Chanticleer Inn** (508-257-6231), also in Siasconset, specializes in French gourmet fare and is considered by many to be the best restaurant on the island. Festive flowers and a brightly painted carousel horse greet diners in the restaurant's garden courtyard, making outdoor dining a must in good weather. The atmosphere, cuisine, and service will cost you, however, as lunch entrées start at around $15, and it would be hard to sit down to dinner for less than $40 per person.

For an elaborate, but pricey, breakfast, try **Arno's** (508-228-5857) on Main Street in Nantucket Center. Arno's has an extensive selection of omelets and breakfast entrées, such as smoked chicken benedict and smoked Norwegian salmon served with herbed eggs, that range from $5.50 to $8.75 each. Breakfast is served daily from 8:00 a.m. to 3:30 p.m. For a more traditional breakfast, try the **Downeyflake** on South Water Street (508-228-4533). They bake terrific homemade doughnuts.

On South Water Street, the **Atlantic Cafe** (508-228-0570) and the **Rose & Crown** (508-228-2595) several doors down both offer satisfying meals in a pub atmosphere. For casual fare, there are numerous fast-food joints on the road leading to the Steamship Authority boat dock. One of them, **Henry's Sandwiches** on Steamboat Wharf (508-228-0123), makes great subs.

Nightlife
Places like the **Rose & Crown** and the **Brotherhood** at 23 Broad Street offer in-town musical entertainment. The **Windsong** (508-228-6900) at the Nantucket Inn on Macy Lane features jazz musicians; the **Box** (508-228-9717) on Daves Street is an informal dance club; and the **Actor's Theatre of Nantucket** performs popular plays throughout the summer (call 508-228-6325 for ticket information).

CAPE COD

Exposed as it is to the ocean, Nantucket tends to get beaten up
occasionally by raging sea storms, yet its quiet, simple life-style
seems sheltered from the outside world. In contrast, the latest
trends in food, fashion, and art somehow manage to make their
way out to Provincetown at the tip of Cape Cod. Once it was a
stopover for the pilgrims. Today the art, gay, and tourist communities all vie for space along Provincetown's harbor, making the
town a hive of activity during the summer months. Journey
from the island of Nantucket to Provincetown, enjoying the
beauty of Cape Cod's National Seashore along the way.

Suggested Schedule

8:00 a.m.	Breakfast.
9:00 a.m.	Spend your last hour and a half on Nantucket visiting a sight you missed the previous day.
10:30 a.m.	Depart for Hyannis.
12:30 p.m.	Arrive in Hyannis and begin journey to Provincetown.
1:00 p.m.	Lunch in Chatham.
2:30 p.m.	Visit the Cape Cod National Seashore.
4:30 p.m.	Travel to Provincetown and check in for the night.
5:30 p.m.	Stroll down Provincetown's colorful Commer- cial Street, perhaps stopping in at the Province- town Heritage or Art Association museums.
7:00 p.m.	Dinner.

Travel Route

The suggested schedule assumes that you are traveling some-
time between mid-June and mid-September. If you are traveling
at any other time of year, the ferry schedule from Nantucket is
much more limited, so you should call either the Steamship
Authority (508-228-0262) or Hy-Line Cruises (508-778-2602)
for departure times during your visit. The Steamship Authority
boat leaves at 10:40 a.m. and doesn't arrive in Hyannis until
1:00 p.m.

From Hyannis, take Route 28 East to Orleans, stopping in the
lovely town of Chatham for lunch. If you have time, visit the
Chatham Lighthouse on Shore Road off Route 28, or drive
down seaside lanes. Some of the Cape's most beautiful homes
are on the ocean in Chatham.

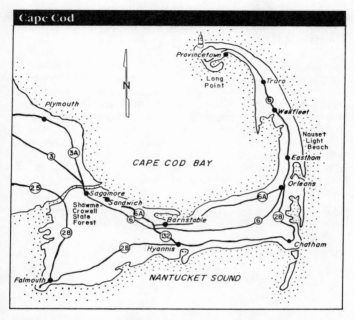

From Chatham, continue on Route 28 to Orleans where
Route 28 intersects with US 6. Follow US 6 to Provincetown.
The Salt Pond Visitor Center off US 6 in Eastham is one of the
main visitor information centers for the Cape Cod National Seashore. At Truro, Route 6A will take you by oceanside motels and
cottages if you're looking for simple beachfront accommodations. US 6 will take you right by the sand dunes.

Sightseeing Highlights
▲▲▲ The Cape Cod National Seashore—The National Seashore stretches from the eastern half of the Cape's elbow all the
way out to its fingertips at Provincetown, offering the visitor
miles of nature trails, beaches, and wind-sculpted sand dunes
peppered with beach grass. You won't be able to cover all
27,000 acres of the seashore in one afternoon, but a ranger at
the Salt Pond Visitor Center can send you off in the direction of
Nauset Lighthouse, a good hiking trail, or a remote beach. The
seashore is open to the public year-round.
In Provincetown, there are several museums where you may
want to spend some time if you're interested in learning more
about Cape Cod history or if poor weather drives you indoors:
▲ Provincetown Art Association and Museum—Changing

exhibits include works by respected American artists such as Milton Avery, as well as promising newcomers to the art scene. The museum at 460 Commercial Street is open daily during the summer from 12:00 p.m. to 4:00 p.m. and then again from 7:00 p.m. to 10:00 p.m. Admission is $1 for adults and $.50 for children and seniors. Call (508) 487-1750 for off-season hours.

▲ **Provincetown Heritage Museum**—Artifacts pertaining to the sea make up the majority of the museum's exhibits, the focal point being the 64-foot-long half-scale model of the *Rose Dorothea*, a turn-of-the-century fishing vessel. It is the largest indoor boat model in the world. Admission to the museum is $2 for adults. Children under 12 years of age are admitted free. The museum is open from 10:00 a.m. to 6:00 p.m. and until 10:00 p.m. during the summer. The museum is on the corner of Commercial and Center streets.

▲ **Pilgrim Monument** and **Provincetown Museum**—You will have no trouble locating the monument because, at 255 feet, it is the tallest all-granite structure in the United States and affords marvelous views of the cape and South Shore on clear days. Museum exhibits spotlight outer Cape Cod history. Unfortunately, handicapped access is limited as there is no elevator to the top of the monument. Visitors must use ramps and stairs to climb to the top. Admission is $2 for adults and $1 for children ages 4 to 12. It is open 9:00 a.m. to 9:00 p.m. during the summer; call (508) 487-1310 for hours if you plan to visit off-season.

Lodging

The Victorian **Anchor Inn** at 175 Commercial Street has a wonderful porch for people-watching, an attractive garden in front, and ocean view rooms that rent for about $100 in summer and $70 off-season (508-487-0432). Rooms not on the ocean are less expensive, and the inn is open throughout the year. Also open year-round is the **White Wind Inn** just across the street. Doubles with private baths go for $55 to $90 during peak months. Call (508) 487-1526 for reservations. The somewhat eclectic **Gabriel's Guestrooms and Apartments** at 104 Bradford Street has a hot tub on the premises, serves continental breakfasts, and has rooms named for Isadora Duncan, Sarah Bernhardt, and Amelia Earhart. Doubles rent for $50 to $100 per night in season, and there is a two-night minimum during the summer, but you might want to try your luck anyway (508-487-3232). The **Somerset Guesthouse** on the corner of Commercial and Pearl streets has very reasonable rates (508-487-0383). All inns listed are convenient to downtown Provincetown.

Route 6A in nearby Truro has a string of cottages and motels on the beach. Accommodations there vary in quality but are an option if you want to stay on the beach or if you are traveling with a family and find in-town bed and breakfasts too expensive for your whole crew. If you have trouble finding lodging in the area, try calling Provincetown's lodging information number, (508) 487-3424, for assistance.

Camping

Coastal Acres Camping Court on the West Vine Street Extension is the closest campground to downtown Provincetown. They do have a three-night minimum stay requirement for reservations, but you could call on the day of your arrival and see if they have space available (508-487-1700). Sites cost $15 for a tent and $20 for RV hookups. **Dune's Edge Campground** off of US 6 is just a little farther from town, but still convenient, and borders on sand dunes of the National Seashore (508-487-9815). In North Truro, there are three campgrounds you might try if Coastal Acres and Dunes Edge are full. They are **Horton's Park** (508-487-1220), **North of Highland Camping Area** (508-487-1191), and **North Truro Camping Area** (508-487-1847).

Dining

For a different sort of dining experience, try **Old Reliable Fish House** at 229 Commercial Street (508-487-9742). It has a mixed menu of Portuguese and Yankee specialties. The restaurant is on the water with outdoor seating in season, and prices are reasonable. **Ciro & Sals** on Kiley Court is known statewide for sumptuous northern Italian creations. Prices are on the high end, and reservations are strongly recommended (508-487-0049). The **Grand Central Cafe** at 5 Masonic Place gives seafood a Mexican treatment with dishes such as lobster enchiladas, shrimp fajitas, and crab chile rellenos. Dinner prices range from $12 to $16 (508-487-9116). The **Fiddleleaf Restaurant**'s menu includes fillet Madagascar, Australian rack of lamb, and veal Alexandra. Dinner entrées start at $20. The brightly painted Victorian structure on Commercial Street is worth a look even if you decide not to dine there. For reservations call (508) 487-1443.

On the more traditional side, **Vorelli's** at 226 Commercial Street serves Italian and seafood dishes in a nice atmosphere. The restaurant also has a raw bar, and dinner entrées range from $14 to $18 (508-487-2778). Also on Commercial Street, the **Mew's** (508-487-1500) and **Pepe's** (508-487-0670) are popular for seafood, while **Cafe Blase** (508-487-9465) serves tasty sandwiches at moderate prices and has a pleasant sidewalk café in the summertime. There is no shortage of sub shops and pizza joints in town, and ice cream lovers are bound to be tempted by **Turner's** wide variety of creamy flavors.

For breakfast, try **Masoltov** on Commercial Street, where omelets go for about $3.50, or **Different Ducks** at 135 Bradford Street for their stuffed doughbabies.

Itinerary Options

If you have more time, the Cape Cod National Seashore has enough beautiful coastline to occupy nature enthusiasts and beach bums alike for many a day. There is always a new dune to investigate. Whale-watching is also an agreeable pastime in this part of the world. *The Portuguese Princess* shuttles eager marine mammal watchers daily from Provincetown, April through November, to view the whales in their natural habitat. Call (508) 487-2651 for ticket information.

PLYMOUTH

In 1620, the pilgrims actually landed in Provincetown first before settling in Plymouth because of its protected harbor. Today you'll follow the pilgrims' path from Provincetown to Plymouth and discover how they survived that first cold winter in America.

Suggested Schedule

9:00 a.m.	Leave Provincetown for Plymouth.
11:00 a.m.	Visit Plymouth Rock and the *Mayflower II*.
12:00 p.m.	Lunch.
1:00 p.m.	Visit Plymouth Plantation.
3:30 p.m.	Visit Cranberry World or another sightseeing highlight of your choice.
5:00 p.m.	Check into lodging.

Travel Route: From Provincetown to Plymouth (85 miles)
From Provincetown, take US 6 to Orleans. At Orleans, get on scenic Route 6A and follow it all the way to the Sagamore Bridge. Route 6A is lined with quaint Cape Cod villages, such as Barnstable and Yarmouth, where you may want to stop along the way. Brewster has lots of antique shops, the Parnassus Book Service in Old Yarmouth is worth a stop, and the Thornton Burgess Society runs the Green Briar Jam Kitchen on Discovery Hill Road off Route 6A in Sandwich. From Sagamore, take Route 3 to the Cedarville Exit and follow Route 3A North to Plymouth.

Sightseeing Highlights
▲ **Plymouth Rock**—There is nothing extraordinary about this enshrined rock other than the fact that it symbolizes the pilgrims' first settlement and thus is a cornerstone of American colonization. Visiting Plymouth Rock is probably comparable to kissing the Blarney Stone; every true patriot should make a pilgrimage there once in a lifetime for their country's sake.
▲▲ **Plimouth Plantation**—The plantation is a living museum exemplifying everyday seventeenth-century pilgrim life and that of seventeenth-century Native Americans in the neighboring Wampanaog Settlement. The plantation also operates the *Mayflower II*, a replica of the ship the pilgrims used to cross the Atlantic in 1620. Costumed guides relate the events of that fateful voyage. The plantation, off Route 3A just south of the town

of Plymouth, and the *Mayflower II*, located at State Pier near Plymouth Rock, are open April through November daily from 9:00 a.m. to 5:00 p.m. The *Mayflower II* is open late, until 6:00 p.m. from mid-June through Labor Day. Admission to the village is $8.50 for adults, $5.25 for children. Admission to the ship is $4.50 for adults, $2.75 for children. Combination tickets are available.

▲ **Cranberry World**—Visit cranberry bogs to see how this bouncy fruit is grown, harvested, and turned into products for everyday consumption. The museum is operated by Ocean Spray. There is no charge for admission, and cranberry refreshments are also free. Cranberry World is located at 225 Water Street in Plymouth and is open from 9:30 a.m. to 5:00 p.m. daily April through November. The center is open until 9:00 p.m. Monday through Friday during July and August.

▲ **Plymouth National Wax Museum**—Overlooking Plymouth Rock and harbor atop Coles Hill, the museum re-creates events in pilgrim history using wax figures. Open daily from 9:00 a.m. to 5:00 p.m. March through November. Admission is $4 for adults and $2 for children.

▲ **Pilgrim Hall Museum**—The museum houses actual personal belongings of the pilgrims, including Governor Bradford's Bible and Myles Standish's sword. The museum is located at 75 Court Street on Route 3A in the center of Plymouth. Admission is $3 for adults, $2.50 for seniors, and $1 for children ages 6 to 15. The museum is open year-round from 9:30 a.m. to 4:30 p.m. daily.

▲ **Cordage Park Marketplace**—The marketplace, now filled with factory outlet stores and boutiques, is of interest because it stands on the site of a nineteenth-century rope manufacturing plant. The Plymouth mill was the world's largest and employed an army of workers. The prints on display throughout the marketplace will give you some sense of the factory's magnitude.

Lodging
The Pilgrim Sands Motel, on Route 3A, is a popular lodging choice because of its oceanfront location and proximity to Plimouth Plantation (508-747-0900). On a smaller scale, **The Colonial House Inn** at 207 Sandwich Street is also convenient to sights and has reasonable rates. Call (508) 746-2087 for reservations. **The Sheraton Plymouth Inn** at 180 Water Street is adjacent to the Village Landing Marketplace not far from Plymouth Rock. Double rooms range from $70 to $100 per night, and it is best to make reservations several weeks ahead during the summer (800-325-3535).

Camping

Indianhead Campground is the closest camping area to Plymouth's attractions off Route 3A, south of Plymouth. The campground has complete hookup and recreational facilities. Call (508) 888-3688 for reservations. **Myles Standish State Forest**, about 10 miles from Plymouth off Route 58 in South Carver, has 475 campsites plus swimming, hiking, boating, and fishing. Call (508) 866-2526 for information.

Dining

McGrath's Harbour Restaurant (508-746-9751) and the **Marina Landing** (508-746-5570) both specialize in seafood and overlook the harbor in downtown Plymouth. **Station One** at 51 Main Street serves a variety of dishes in an agreeable setting. The building was constructed in the early 1900s as a fire station (508-746-6001). For fast-food, try the food pavilion at the Cordage Park Marketplace.

THE SOUTH SHORE

Today brings you full circle to Boston where your 22-day journey began. If you have time, drive through the pretty seaside villages of Duxbury, Hingham, and Cohasset, then perhaps visit the John F. Kennedy Memorial Library for an in-depth look at a president whose youth, charisma, and promise were so influential in shaping modern history.

Suggested Schedule

8:00 a.m.	Breakfast.
9:00 a.m.	Leave Plymouth for Boston traveling along Massachusetts' South Shore.
12:00 p.m.	Lunch in Cohasset.
1:00 p.m.	Explore Hingham and World's End Reservation.
2:00 p.m.	Visit the Adams National Historic Site in Quincy.
3:30 p.m.	Visit the John F. Kennedy Memorial Library.
5:00 p.m.	Return to Boston.

Travel Route: Plymouth to Boston (40 miles)

Today's schedule assumes you are not rushing back to catch a plane. If you are, take Route 3 North to Interstate 93 North directly to Boston. The trip will take about an hour, or longer in traffic.

To return to Boston in a more leisurely fashion, take Route 3A North from Plymouth. Route 3A merges with Route 3 briefly, so be sure to exit for the Duxburys at 3A to continue on the coastal route. Route 3A will take you through the towns of Duxbury, Marshfield, Cohasset, and Hingham, but the nicest houses and best views of the ocean are off the highway. In these towns, I recommend taking back road detours to investigate the villages more thoroughly.

True to its name, Marshfield has two wildlife sanctuaries in marshy habitats, the North River Wildlife Sanctuary and the Daniel Webster Wildlife Sanctuary. In Duxbury, you might want to seek out the John Alden House at 105 Alden Street or the Old Burying Ground on Chestnut Street where Myles Standish is buried along with other passengers from the *Mayflower*. In Cohasset, be sure to drive out to the harbor. In Hingham, there is the World's End Reservation, 250 acres of shoreline park

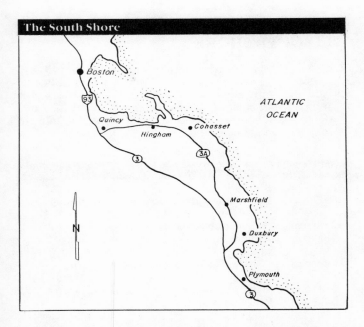

The South Shore

designed by Frederick Law Olmstead, whose work you've seen in the Boston Public Gardens.

In Quincy, follow signs to the Adams National Historic Site. Then return to Route 3A, which will take you to Interstate 93 North. To get to the Kennedy Library, take Exit 14 off of I-93 to Morrissey Boulevard. Follow signs to the library. After visiting the library, get back on I-93 North to Boston, to the airport, or to wherever your next destination lies.

Sightseeing Highlights
▲ **Adams National Historic Site**—The site is actually comprised of houses at several different locations that were the homes and birthplaces of U.S. presidents John Adams and John Quincy Adams, writers Henry and Brook Adams, and envoy Charles Adams. The tour of the home at 135 Adams Street is the most worthwhile of the three. Tour guides provide in-depth historical background information to go along with family artifacts, and I especially enjoyed the library. The house is open for tours daily from 9:00 a.m. to 5:00 p.m. mid-April through mid-November. If you wish to see the birthplaces as well, the tour guides can provide you with directions. One admission fee of $2 will admit you to all the homes. Children under 16 years of age are admitted free of charge.

▲▲ **John F. Kennedy Memorial Library**—Don't let the term "library" keep you from going because you think you're going to see only books. In an imposing building designed by noted architect I. M. Pei overlooking the ocean, your visit begins with a film on Kennedy. Then it's on to the exhibits, which include Kennedy's presidential desk and a time line juxtaposing Kennedy memorabilia, events in his life, and major events of the day. More than just a tribute to one man, the library gives you a fascinating look at our recent past. It also is a thought-provoking way to end the trip, since it provides you with a point of reference to judge modern America against the dreams of our founding fathers whose ideals have become apparent during the past three weeks. The library is open daily from 9:00 a.m. to 5:00 p.m., closing only for Thanksgiving, Christmas, and New Year's Day. The last film of the day starts at 3:50 p.m. Admission is charged.

Dining
Hugo's Lighthouse Restaurant overlooking the water in Cohasset is known for its seafood and might be a good place to stop for lunch if you're not picnicking (617-383-1700).

Back in Boston
Boston will seem like an old friend as the city's skyline comes into view upon your return. The city is worth getting to know better if other obligations are not calling you home. If you must leave the area, New England's charms are certain to beckon you back for another visit.

FESTIVALS AND EVENTS

Each New England state has its share of folk festivals ranging from arts and crafts fairs to lobsterfests. These regional events are a fun way to soak up local culture, and I've listed some of the area's best and most colorful below.

Connecticut
May
Lobster Festival, Mystic Seaport Museum, Mystic.
August
Railroad Days, Canaan.
Governor's Cup Regatta, Connecticut River and Long Island Sound, Essex.
Native American Festival, Haddam Meadows State Park, Haddam.
September
Harbor Festival, New London.
October
Chowder Days, Mystic Seaport Museum, Mystic.
December
Festival of Light, Constitution Plaza, Hartford.
Victorian Christmas, Gillette Castle State Park, Hadlyme.
Christmas at Mystic Seaport, Mystic.
Call (203) 566-3948, or write Travel Office, Department of Economic Development, 210 Washington Street, Hartford, CT 06106, for a complete list of Connecticut events.

Maine
January
New Year's Eve Celebration, Portland.
Happy New Year's Champagne Cup, Sunday River Ski Area, Bethel.
June
Old Port Festival, Old Port, Portland.
July
Seafood Festival, Bar Harbor.
Great Schooner Race, Rockland Harbor, Rockland.
Annual Dulcimer Festival, Bar Harbor.
Rockport Folk Festival, Rockport.
Arcady Music Festival, Mt. Desert.
August
Lobster Festival, Rockland.
Maine Arts Festival, Portland.

December
Christmas Prelude, Kennebunkport.
Contact the Maine Publicity Bureau at 97 Winthrop Street, Hallowell, ME 04347 (207-289-2423), for the most current events calendar.

Massachusetts
January
First Night New Year's Eve Celebration, Boston.
March
St. Patrick's Day Parade, South Boston.
April
The Boston Marathon, Boston.
July
Boston Pops Concert and Fourth of July Fireworks Display, The Esplanade, Boston.
Harborfest, Boston.
August
Annual Festival of Shaker Crafts and Industries, Hancock Shaker Village.
September
Eastern States Exposition, West Springfield.
October
Head of the Charles Regatta, Charles River, Cambridge.
Mt. Greylock Ramble, Adams.
December
Christmas Stroll, Nantucket.
Whale of a Christmas Celebration, Edgartown, Martha's Vineyard.
For more information on "Bay state" festivals, contact the Commonwealth of Massachusetts Office of Travel and Tourism, 100 Cambridge Street, 13th Floor, Boston, MA 02202.

New Hampshire
May
Mountainfest, Mt. Washington Valley.
June
Mt. Washington Road Race, Mt. Washington.
Old Timers Fair, Hanover.
Annual Fiddler's Contest, Lincoln.
Jazz Festival, Portsmouth.
July
Mid-Summer Arts and Crafts Fair, Loon Mountain, Lincoln.

August
Mt. Washington Valley Road Rally, North Conway.
September
World Mud Bowl Championships, Hog Coliseum, North
   Conway.
Autumn Leaves Square Dance Festival, Cannon Mountain,
   Franconia.
Railfans Day, Conway Scenic Railroad, North Conway.
Miles to Isles Windsurfing Regatta, Portsmouth.
Highland Games, Loon Mountain, Lincoln.
October
Fall Foliage Festival, Loon Mountain, Lincoln.
For more detailed information on New Hampshire festivals,
   contact the State of New Hampshire, Office of Vacation
   Travel, P.O. Box 856-RC, Concord, NH 03301 (603-271-2666).

Rhode Island
January
Polar Bears Dip, New Year's Day, Newport Beach, Newport.
March
Irish Heritage Month, Newport.
April
Newport Surfing Championship, Middletown.
May
Newport Fun Cup Sailboarding Regatta, Fort Adams, Newport.
Jaguar Festival, Newport Yachting Center, Newport.
June
Secret Garden Tour, Newport.
New York Yacht Club Regatta, Newport.
Block Island Race Week, Block Island.
International Multi-hull Festival, Newport.
July
Virginia Slims Tennis Tournament, Newport Casino, Newport.
Black Ships Festival, Newport.
Newport Music Festival, Newport Mansions.
August
New England Regional Croquet Tournament, Newport Casino,
   Newport.
The International Jumping Derby, Glen Farm, Portsmouth.
JVC Jazz Festival at Newport, Fort Adams.
September
Ocean State Maritime Week, Newport.
October
Aquidneck Island Harvest Fair, Middletown.
November
Ocean State Marathon, Newport.

December

Christmas in Newport, Newport.
Call or write the Newport Tourism and Convention Authority,
P.O. Box 782, Newport, RI 02840 (401-849-8048), for a free
descriptive brochure of Newport County's numerous cultural
events.

Vermont

June

Hot Air Balloon Festival, Quechee.

July

Summer Film Festival, Southern Vermont Art Center, Manchester.
Volvo Tennis Tournament, Stratton Mountain.

August

Vermont State Craft Fair, Killington.
Bennington Battle Day Weekend, Bennington.

September

Vermont State Fair, Rutland.
Wurstfest, Stratton Mountain.
Southern Vermont Festival of Fools, Hildene Meadowlands,
Manchester.
The Vermont Chamber of Commerce, Box 37, Montpelier,
VT 05602 (802-223-3443), can provide you with additional
information about ongoing activities and events in the state.

Maine
Snow Bowl in Camden (207-236-3438) is a small mountain offering pleasant skiing for the whole family. **Sunday River** in Bethel (207-824-2187) is more extensive with 50 trails and a 1,854-foot vertical drop.

Massachusetts
Butternut Basin in Great Barrington (413-528-2000), **Catamount** in South Egremont (413-528-1262), **Jiminy Peak** in Hancock (413-738-5500), and **Brodie Mountain** in New Ashford (413-443-4752) are all in the Berkshire region of the state and provide skiing terrain for all levels of ability. Brodie has the greatest vertical drop at 1,250 feet, while Catamount straddles the Massachusetts and New York border. Brodie and Butternut both have cross-country trails as well.

New Hampshire
There is a heavy concentration of ski areas in the Mt. Washington valley. **Black Mountain** in Jackson (603-383-4490) and **Mt. Cranmore** in North Conway (603-356-5543) are good family mountains, since they cater to all levels of ability. Mt. Cranmore's skimobile tramway is a godsend to those scared of chairlifts. **Attitash** in Bartlett (603-374-2369 or 1-800-862-1600), **Wildcat** opposite the Mt. Washington Auto Road (603-466-3326), **Cannon** in Franconia (603-823-5563), and **Loon Mountain** in Lincoln (603-745-8111) offer experienced skiers more of a challenge. Wildcat and Loon both have gondolas, and Cannon operates an aerial tramway. **Bretton Woods** near the cog railway to the top of Mt. Washington is best known for its cross-country trails (603-278-1000), and the town of Jackson is also a major cross-country center—contact the Jackson Ski Touring Foundation at (603) 383-9355 for information. **Tuckerman's Ravine** at Pinkham Notch is only for the most adventurous and expert skiers. There are no lifts so skiers must hike two and a half miles. Check with the White Mountain National Forest Service before trying to tackle the ravine.

Vermont
Killington (802-773-1500), with 100 trails and a 3,081-foot vertical drop, is the largest ski area discussed here. Nearby **Pico** (802-775-4345) outside of Rutland is also an enjoyable place to ski. **Bromley** in Manchester (802-824-5522) has 35 trails and **Stratton** (802-297-2200), 20 minutes away, is a popular ski resort as well.

OTHER BOOKS FROM JOHN MUIR PUBLICATIONS

22 Days Series: Travel Itinerary Planners
These pocket-size guides are a refreshing departure from ordinary guidebooks.
Each author has in-depth knowledge of the region covered and offers 22
carefully tested daily itineraries. Included are not only "must see" attractions
but also little-known villages and hidden "jewels" as well as valuable general
information. 128 to 144 pp., $7.95 each
22 Days in Alaska by Pamela Lanier (28-68-0)
22 Days in the American Southwest by Richard Harris (28-88-5)
22 Days in Asia by Roger Rapoport and Burl Willes (65-17-3)
22 Days in Australia by John Gottberg (65-03-3)
22 Days in California by Roger Rapoport (28-93-1)
22 Days in China by Gaylon Duke and Zenia Victor (28-72-9)
22 Days in Europe by Rick Steves (65-05-X)
22 Days in France by Rick Steves (65-07-6)
22 Days in Germany, Austria & Switzerland by Rick Steves (65-02-5)
22 Days in Great Britain by Rick Steves (28-67-2)
22 Days in Hawaii by Arnold Schuchter (28-92-3)
22 Days in India by Anurag Mathur (28-87-7)
22 Days in Japan by David Old (28-73-7)
22 Days in Mexico by Steve Rogers and Tina Rosa (65-04-1)
22 Days in New England by Anne E. Wright (28-96-6)
22 Days in New Zealand by Arnold Schuchter (28-86-9)
22 Days in Norway, Denmark & Sweden by Rick Steves (28-83-4)
22 Days in the Pacific Northwest by Richard Harris (28-97-4)
22 Days in Spain & Portugal by Rick Steves (65-06-8)
22 Days in the West Indies by Cyndy and Sam Morreale (28-74-5)

"Kidding Around" Travel Guides for Children
Written for kids eight years of age and older. Generously illustrated in two
colors with imaginative characters and images. Each guide is an adventure to
read and a treasure to keep.
Kidding Around San Francisco, Rosemary Zibart (65-23-8) 64 pp., $9.95
Kidding Around Washington, D.C., Anne Pedersen (65-25-4) 64 pp., $9.95
Kidding Around London, Sarah Lovett (65-24-6) 64 pp., $9.95

All-Suite Hotel Guide: The Definitive Directory, Pamela Lanier
Pamela Lanier, author of The Complete Guide to Bed & Breakfasts, Inns &
Guesthouses, now provides the discerning traveler with a listing of over 600
all-suite hotels. (65-08-4) 285 pp., $13.95

Asia Through the Back Door, Rick Steves and John Gottberg
Provides information and advice you won't find elsewhere—including how to
overcome culture shock, bargain in marketplaces, observe Buddhist temple
etiquette, and even how to eat noodles with chopsticks! (28-58-3) 336 pp.,
$11.95

Buddhist America: Centers, Practices, Retreats, Don Morreale
The only comprehensive directory of Buddhist centers, this guide includes
first-person narratives of individuals' retreat experiences. (28-94-X) 312 pp.,
$12.95

Bus Touring: Charter Vacations, U.S.A., Stuart Warren with Douglas Bloch
For many people, bus touring is the ideal, relaxed, and comfortable way to see America. Covers every aspect of bus touring to help passengers get the most pleasure for their money. (28-95-8) 200 pp., $9.95

Catholic America: Self-Renewal Centers and Retreats, Patricia Christian-Meyers
Complete directory of over 500 self-renewal centers and retreats in the United States and Canada. (65-20-3) 325 pp., $13.95

Complete Guide to Bed & Breakfasts, Inns & Guesthouses in the United States and Canada, 1989-90 Edition, Pamela Lanier
Newly revised and the most complete directory available, with over 5,000 listings in all 50 states, 10 Canadian provinces, Puerto Rico, and the U.S. Virgin Islands. (65-09-2) 520 pp., $14.95

Elegant Small Hotels: A Connoisseur's Guide, Pamela Lanier
This lodging guide for discriminating travelers describes hotels characterized by exquisite rooms and suites and personal service par excellence. (65-10-6) 230 pp., $14.95

Europe 101: History & Art for the Traveler, Rick Steves and Gene Openshaw
The first and only jaunty history and art book for travelers makes castles, palaces, and museums come alive. (28-78-8) 372 pp., $12.95

Europe Through the Back Door, Rick Steves
For people who want to enjoy Europe more and spend less money doing it. In this revised edition, Steves shares more of his well-respected insights. (28-84-2) 404 pp., $12.95
Doubleday and Literary Guild Book Club Selection.

Gypsying After 40: A Guide to Adventure and Self-Discovery, Bob Harris
Retirees Bob and Megan Harris offer a witty and informative guide to the "gypsying" life-style that has enriched their lives and can enrich yours. Their message is: "Anyone can do it!" (28-71-0) 312 pp., $12.95

The Heart of Jerusalem, Arlynn Nellhaus
Arlynn Nellhaus draws on her vast experience in and knowledge of Jerusalem to give travelers a rare inside view and practical guide to the Golden City. (28-79-6) 312 pp., $12.95

Mona Winks: Self-Guided Tours of Europe's Top Museums, Rick Steves and Gene Openshaw
Here's a guide that will save you time, shoe leather, and tired muscles. It is designed for people who want to get the most out of visiting the great museums of Europe. (28-85-0) 450 pp., $14.95

The On and Off the Road Cookbook, Carl Franz and Lorena Havens
A multitude of delicious alternatives to the usual campsite meals. (28-27-3) 272 pp., $8.50

The People's Guide to Mexico, Carl Franz
This classic guide shows the traveler how to handle just about any situation that might arise while in Mexico.
"The best 360-degree coverage of traveling and short-term living in Mexico that's going." — *Whole Earth Epilog* (28-99-0) 587 pp., $14.95

The People's Guide to RV Camping in Mexico, Carl Franz and Lorena Havens
This revised guide focuses on the special pleasures and challenges of RV travel in Mexico. Includes a complete campground directory. (28-91-5) 304 pp., $13.95

The Shopper's Guide to Mexico, Steve Rogers and Tina Rosa
The only comprehensive handbook for shopping in Mexico, this guide ferrets out little-known towns where the finest handicrafts are made and offers tips on shopping techniques. (28-90-7) 200 pp., $9.95

Traveler's Guide to Asian Culture, Kevin Chambers
An accurate and enjoyable guide to the history and culture of this diverse continent. (65-14-9) 356 pp., $13.95

Traveler's Guide to Healing Centers and Retreats in North America, Martine Rudee and Jonathan Blease
Over 300 listings offer a wide range of healing centers—from traditional to new age. (65-15-7) 224 pp., $11.95

Undiscovered Islands of the Caribbean, Burl Willes
For the past decade, Burl Willes has been tracking down remote Caribbean getaways. Here he offers complete information on 32 islands. (28-80-X) 220 pp., $12.95

Automotive Repair Manuals
Each JMP automotive manual gives clear step-by-step instructions together with illustrations that show exactly how each system in the vehicle comes apart and goes back together. They tell everything a novice or experienced mechanic needs to know to perform periodic maintenance, tune-ups, troubleshooting, and repair of the brake, fuel and emission control, electrical, cooling, clutch, transmission, driveline, steering and suspension systems and even rebuild the engine.
How to Keep Your VW Alive (65-12-2) 410 pp., $17.95
How to Keep Your Golf/Jetta/Rabbit Alive (65-21-1) 420 pp., $17.95
How to Keep Your Honda Car Alive (28-55-9) 272 pp., $17.95
How to Keep Your Subaru Alive (65-11-4) 420 pp., $17.95
How to Keep Your Toyota Pick-Up Alive (28-89-3) 400 pp., $17.95
How to Keep Your Datsun/Nissan Alive (28-65-6) 544 pp., $17.95
How to Keep Your Honda ATC Alive (28-45-1) 236 pp., $14.95

Other Automotive Books

The Greaseless Guide to Car Care Confidence: Take the Terror out of Talking to Your Mechanic, Mary Jackson
Teaches the reader about all of the basic systems of an automobile. (65-19-X) 200 pp., $14.95

Off-Road Emergency Repair & Survival, James Ristow
Glove compartment guide to troubleshooting, temporary repair, and survival. (65-26-2) 150 pp., $9.95

Road & Track's Used Car Classics, edited by Peter Bohr
Features over 70 makes and models of enthusiast cars built between 1953 and 1979. (28-69-9) 272 pp., $12.95

Ordering Information

Fill in the order blank. Be sure to add up all of the subtotals at the bottom of the order form and give us the address whither your order is to be whisked.

Postage & Handling

Your books will be sent to you via UPS (for U.S. destinations), and you will receive them in approximately 10 days from the time that we receive your order. Include $2.75 for the first item ordered and $.50 for each additional item to cover shipping and handling costs. UPS shipments to post office boxes take longer to arrive; if possible, please give us a street address.

For airmail within the U.S., enclose $4.00 per book for shipping and handling.

All foreign orders will be shipped surface rate. Please enclose $3.00 for the first item and $1.00 for each additional item. Please inquire for airmail rates.

Method of Payment

Your order may be paid by check, money order, or credit card. We cannot be responsible for cash sent through the mail.

All payments must be made in U.S. dollars drawn on a U.S. bank. Canadian postal money orders in U.S. dollars are also acceptable.

For VISA, MasterCard, or American Express orders, use the order form or call (505)982-4078. Books ordered on American Express cards can be shipped only to the billing address of the cardholder. Sorry, no C.O.D.'s. Residents of sunny New Mexico, add 5.625% tax to the total.

Back Orders

We will back order all forthcoming and out-of-stock titles unless otherwise requested.

All prices subject to change without notice.

Address all orders and inquiries to: **John Muir Publications**
P.O. Box 613
Santa Fe, NM 87504   **(505)982-4078**

ITEM NO.		TITLE	EACH	QUAN.	TOTAL
	·				
	·				
	·				
	·				
	·				

Postage & handling (see ordering information)* _____

New Mexicans please add 5.625% tax _____

Total Amount Due _____

Credit Card Number: _____

Expiration Date: _____ Daytime telephone _____

Name _____

Address _____

City _____ State _____ Zip _____

Signature X _____

Required for Credit Card Purchases